SURRENDERED

This book is set in the typeface Athelas designed by Veronika Burian and Jose Scaglione.

Paperback ISBN: 978-1-955546-32-4
Hardcover ISBN: 978-1-088035-42-9

A Publication of *Tall Pine Books*
119 E Center Street, Suite B4A | Warsaw, Indiana 46580
www.tallpinebooks.com

| 1 23 23 20 16 02 |

Published in the United States of America

SURRENDERED

DISCOVERING GOD'S WILL *for* YOUR LIFE!

DEBRA A. ELROD

This book is dedicated to:

This book is only made possible because of God the Father, Jesus Christ, and the work of the Holy Spirit in my life. My gratitude goes to all of my family, friends, brothers, and sisters in Christ who came alongside me during this journey, but especially to the ones who were closest—my daughters who walked through the most difficult of times with me and my husband—who the Lord sent to take my hand and lead me back into the world I had checked out of. To the believers who came along my journey early on to disciple me in the Word, I'm forever grateful. It drew me closer to the Lord in prayer, His Word, and hearing from the Holy Spirit, to be still and know that He is God!

CONTENTS

INTRODUCTION

IF YOU'RE CONSIDERING reading this book, there's no doubt it's God who is calling you into a relationship with Him of complete surrender! It doesn't matter who you are—leader, pastor, mother, father, employer, employee, student, or child—God wants you to surrender it all to Him! "Come to me all you who labor and are heavy laden and I will give you rest" (Matthew 11:28 NKJV). I can tell you from personal knowledge and experience, it's only when you surrender your life completely that you will find your life! "If you cling to your life, you will lose it; but if you give it up for me, you will find it" (Matthew 10:39 NLT).

That's exactly what happened to me. This book is a culmination of finding my life as I surrendered at the cross of Jesus Christ. Jesus brought a sword! He separated me from ungodly, toxic relationships and delivered me from religious idolatry, chasing after the American dream, and demonic oppression, possession, and infiltration. He freed me from the bondage of sinful behavior that I was powerless to change on the inside. He brought peace to my mind and soul from demonic attacks endured since early child-

hood and passed down from prior generations. He "miraculous-
ly" changed me from the inside out! Because I knew this change
was really happening within me, it inspired me to continue moving forward in spite of relentless opposition. I was descending naturally, but ascending spiritually! My mind was fixed on trusting in
God alone to deliver me out of it! When the Holy Spirit said, "Turn
here," I did, and when He said to do this or do that, I walked very
close to Jesus, hearing from Him daily.

The first seven years of my journey were spent studying, learning, and memorizing scriptures, with four of those years of intense
study. I would talk with long-time believers and wonder why they
weren't "getting it." One day, I said, "Lord, what's going on here?
Why am I knowing this and they are not?" He answered in my spirit, "You are on O.B.T." (On the Bible Training). I wasn't just reading and studying the Bible; I was living it! In fact, there were times
when I not only needed it to get through the day but the next minute! The Bible was tied to me like a life jacket, very close. If it had
not been, I wouldn't be here to tell you about it.

This is a journey I never planned for myself. My goal was to
climb the corporate ladder to get to the top of the automotive manufacturing industry, but God planned to bring me much higher!
I've come to a place in my life where if the glory of God isn't in it,
then I'm not interested. He changed my desires to align with His
chosen purpose for my life. He wants to do the same for you! I
won't pretend it was easy because it wasn't. I walked through hell
a couple of times, but Jesus walked through with me (Psalm 23). I
will be as transparent and forthright as possible as I share the most
remarkable journey I've ever experienced in my life! I was transferred from the Kingdom of Darkness to the Kingdom of Light.
Knowing who I am in Christ changed my life forever! Yes, I still
have battles, but I know today the battle belongs to the Lord, and
He will not allow the righteous to be overtaken. I knew writing this

book would bring more attacks (and it has), but I'm confident the Lord is with me and has equipped and prepared me to share this truth with you. As you read, I hope you are encouraged to surrender all! Don't wait another moment; start right NOW! Pray and ask the Lord to open your heart and mind to receive His will for your life as we journey together through Surrendered.

Father God, I ask for you to open my heart and mind to your Truth and Word! Help me to see what I can't see and hear what I don't hear. Help me today to surrender my entire life and follow the leading of the Holy Spirit to discover Your will for my life. I ask this in the name of Jesus, Amen!

Thank you for going on this journey of Surrendered with me! Have you ever wanted to ask the author a question about their book? Here's your opportunity!

Also, as a special thanks I'd like to give you a free gift, "Tips on living a daily Surrendered life" sent to your email box.

To ask a question and/or claim your free gift, go to www.narrowgatenow.com , Contact Us page, "Ask the Author."

Blessing to you,

Debra Elrod

CHAPTER ONE

SURRENDER

DISCOVERING GOD'S WILL FOR YOUR LIFE THROUGH SURRENDER.

EVERYONE WANTS TO know God's will for their life. When you are seeking God's will with all of your heart, you are in His will and on your way. "You will seek Me and find Me when you search for me with all your heart" (Jeremiah 29:13 NIV, emphasis added).

> "Ask and it will be given to you, seek and you will find; knock and the door will be opened to you. For everyone who asks receives; the one who seeks finds; and the one who knocks, the door will be opened" (Matthew 7:7-8 NIV).

Surrendering your life to the lordship of Jesus Christ is the beginning of discovering the life you were created to live. God's will for your life will emerge as you surrender.

One night, in February of 2005, while looking at the Bible sitting on my nightstand, I said to myself, "I'm going to read this Bible from beginning to end and see if the answers for life are in here." The first thought that came into my mind was, "The answers for life are not in the Bible." Then I looked at my hand and said to myself, "Then how was my hand made? How did I get here? Why am I even living?" I certainly wasn't finding the answers in my business books or even Christian books that all point to the Bible. So, I decided to read it, and if the answers for life weren't in there, at least I can say I've read it. I started at the beginning of Genesis, and it wasn't long into the reading that I found some events to be questionable. I thought, "Did these things really happen? Well, things are happening today that most people wouldn't believe, so who is to say it didn't happen?" I decided to accept it as a possibility and kept reading. While reading in the book of Proverbs, the first scripture that really stood out to me was in chapter three: "Trust in the Lord with all your heart; do not depend on your own understanding. Seek His will in all you do, and He will direct your paths" (Proverbs 3:5-6 NLT). I thought this was good and wrote it in a journal. "For the profit of wisdom is better than silver and her wages are better than gold. Wisdom is more precious than rubies, nothing you desire can compare with her" (Proverbs 3:14-15 NLT). I pondered this scripture and thought that if nothing I desire compares with wisdom, then I better start getting wisdom. What is wisdom? A few chapters later it was written, "The fear of the Lord is the beginning of wisdom, and the knowledge of the Holy One is understanding" (Proverbs 9:10 NLT). It was clear to me that wisdom was going to be found in the pages of the Bible. The more I read and journaled, the more the Bible became real in my life. Ten months later, I surrendered to God completely!

What does "surrender" to God really look like? We might ask ourselves a range of questions. Is surrender a religious activity? What will I have to give up to surrender? How will my life change once I surrender? I am a Christian, so doesn't that mean I have already surrendered? The answer to these questions and others is revealed by the Holy Spirit, in the Word of God, and through our personal testimony. Let's journey together!

IS SURRENDER A RELIGIOUS ACTIVITY?

There was a time in my life when I thought I knew Jesus from my indoctrinated childhood religion. I thought I had a front-row seat in heaven. I thought all other Christian religions were doing it the wrong way. But a tragic event in my early twenties would lead me to question my denominational loyalty. After the death of a close friend through suicide and even contemplating it myself, I cried out to God, "WHY DID YOU DROP ME HERE TO NOT GIVE ANSWERS FOR MY LIFE? I'M NOT CHECKING OUT UNTIL YOU DO!" I went to a local church to talk to the leader. When I sat in his office, tears pouring out of my eyes, I confessed every sin I ever committed and shared about my friend's suicide. When I was done, the first thing he said was, "Why did you come here?" This was not the response I was expecting. My instant reply was, "That's a good question. I don't know, but thank you very much, I probably shouldn't have." And I got up to leave. He tried to stop me, but it was too late. I dried up my tears, got into my car, looked up to heaven, and said, "Now what do I do?" This was the first time in my life ever considering attending a non-denominational church. During the first Sunday service, the pastor made an altar call to give your life to Jesus so that you can have a new life. I thought that is exactly what I needed, a new life, and they were not offering that in my church. I thought, "This is the ticket. I'm going up to the altar and don't care who sees it or what they think!" I needed a change in my life and knew it had to come from above because no one on Earth could help me. While at the altar, I prayed the sinner's prayer, something like this: "Lord Jesus, I confess I am a sinner and have sinned against You and You alone. Please forgive me for my sins. I believe You are the Son of God and that You died for my sins. I believe You were raised from the dead and are seated at the right hand of the Father. Come into my heart and cleanse me from my sins and change me. I ask this in the name of Jesus, Amen."

I looked around at the people at the altar, expecting something miraculous to happen, but nothing! I didn't feel a thing and went back to my seat. I continued attending the church, hoping something would happen eventually. One Sunday, the pastor was preaching passionately, and the congregation was responding with "Amens" and "Hallelujahs," and it was growing more intense! I knew something was going on but didn't know what and all of a sudden, as if on "cue," the preaching stopped. Everyone was silent and kneeling, except for one woman who started praying out loud in a "language" I did not understand. As I was kneeling like everyone else, I thought, "This is it. These people are crazy. I'm out of here." Years later as I read the Scriptures, I could hardly believe it was exactly my experience. "Even so, if unbelievers or people who don't understand these things come into your church meeting and hear everyone speaking in an unknown language, they will think you are crazy" (1 Corinthians 14:23 NLT).

It takes more than a walk to the altar and a prayer to come to complete surrender, but it is a start. God sees into our hearts and knows our true motives. It is not religious activities that will bring you to surrender, as we will discover.

WHAT WILL I HAVE TO GIVE UP TO SURRENDER?

When marriage and children came along, I retreated to what I knew best, my childhood religion, and was satisfied with the weekly church experience. But the Holy Spirit continued witnessing to me as I continued reading through the Bible. In the book of Exodus, it was uncanny how Moses was experiencing very similar people issues in his day, as I was in leading my small business. "Then the people turned against Moses. 'What are we going to drink?' They demanded" (Exodus 15: 24 NLT). There, too, the whole community of Israel spoke bitterly against Moses and Aaron. "Oh, that we were back in Egypt," they moaned. "It would have been better if the Lord had killed us there! At least there we had plenty to eat. But now you have brought us into this desert to starve us to death" (Exodus 16: 2-3 NLT). The similarities were astounding to me. Whether in Moses' day or my business, the people were always complaining about something, whether they didn't make enough money or get enough vacation, personal or sick days. No matter what, they were never getting enough. Then I read where Moses' father-in-law gives him advice on delegating to better manage the large number of people. You can read it in Exodus 18. I thought, "Wow, the delegation of authority began with Moses, not the industrial revolution as taught in business school."

During this time, I hired an independent salesman. In a training session, he said, "I see something in you that is unbelievable. I'm comparing you to Moses." I laughed and said, "Moses, really?" This raised my curiosity about Moses. Before reading the Bible that night, I had a conversation with God and said, "You know, Lord we're all corrupt. You should just wipe us all out, myself included." "Then the Lord said, 'I have seen how stubborn and rebellious these people are. Now leave me alone so my anger can blaze against them and destroy them all. Then I will make you, Moses, into a great nation instead of them.' But Moses pleaded with the Lord his God not to do it" (Exodus 32:9-11a NLT). I was amazed and said to myself, "My goodness! I'm not God! How could I have said the same thing God said?" When I was back at the office, I told the salesman, "Luckily, for you and me, I'm not Moses, because we all would have been taken out!"

Around this time, a business opportunity presented itself to catapult my company sales into the multimillion-dollar range. An experience I had the prior year came to my memory. While sitting in the great room of my home looking around, I thought, "I should be shouting for joy with the life I am living and since I'm not, maybe when I have a 10 million or 100 million or even a billion-dollar business, then I will be overjoyed." I heard a whisper in my ear clearly say, "No, whether you have a 10 million or 1 billion-dollar business, you are going to find yourself right back here!" Remembering this, I said, "Lord, don't let me get to the end of my life having accumulated all this wealth and missing out on what life is really about." Jesus and the Holy Spirit went to work. Investment money was needed to get this new business opportunity off the ground, but everywhere I turned there was a wall of opposition. My customer base began increasing orders to meet the need and then a wrong order issued by the customer got the attention of a high-level director who ceased all orders to my company. Ironically, this would have been an easy roadblock to push through, but not this time! I did everything humanly possible and had the backing of the customers, but this director was not budging. It was becoming surreal, and I instinctively remember saying to myself, "This is not a man stopping me or even the devil. This is God Himself." God gifted me to be a moneymaker, and if my finances were drying up, it was God Himself doing it. So, I decided to sit back, and wait to see what God was doing!

There were times I just wanted to dig a hole the size of a coffin and lay down in it! I was encouraged to start listening to a well-known female preacher on the radio. After a few months of listening to her while driving to a customer appointment, at the end of her message, she said, "I'm talking to someone out there, and like

Moses, God wants you to lay your "scepter" down so that when you pick it back up, you will have real power!" As soon as she said the name, Moses, I knew God was talking to me through her. Tears started coming down my face. I cried out, "Lord, I know You're talking to me. I don't know how to lay it down; You are going to have to lay it down for me!" Not long after, this scripture captured my heart: "You can enter God's Kingdom only through the narrow gate. The highway to hell is broad and its gate is wide for the many who choose the easy way. But the gateway to life is small, and the road is narrow and only a few ever find it" (Matthew 7:13-14 NLT). During regularly scheduled meetings with business associates, customers, and employees, I would share about getting through the "Narrow Gate" and of all the things we can accomplish in life, getting through this gate is the most important and should be our top priority, and it was mine!

On December 7, 2005, while driving to my office, I started having an intense conversation with God about the issues I was facing in my life at the time. I said, "I know the Bible contains every answer for living, and I'm sorry that I never read it for myself, but I CAN'T CRAM FOR THIS EXAM! I don't know what to do. I need You to tell me what to do. I will do whatever You say, because I know you know what's best. While pointing to Heaven, I shouted out in desperation, "BUT YOU HAVE TO BE THE ONE TO TELL ME WHAT TO DO!" These words weren't even off of my lips when to my amazement, He answered! He sent a vision in my head that was very alarming. I saw myself bowed down in the presence of God, in submission with my right arm covering my head! I had this sense that he took His finger and touched my tongue and I never wanted to say another swear word again. I also felt this great sense of calm and peace enter me as a heaviness was lifted. I smelled the scent of burning incense coming through my car vents. When I looked up into the sky at a stoplight, the sun appeared to me as if it were dancing, moving up and down and to the sides rapidly. I knew what was happening to me was out of this world, and I thought, "If I tell anyone this, they will think I am crazy and have me committed!" I didn't correlate this experience at the time with being born again or saved, as it wasn't familiar to me. But this was the moment I came to true repentance, surrendered my life to the lordship of Jesus Christ, and was born again! This was an awakening, unlike anything I had ever experienced. It was on this day I was transferred from the Kingdom of Darkness to the Kingdom of Light, filled with the Holy Spirit, and my life would never be the same again.

What did I give up? My own way! Acknowledging through repentance that it was God who had all the answers written in the Bible. "Repent therefore and be converted, that your sins may be blotted out, so that times of refreshing may come from the presence of the Lord" (Acts 3:19 NKJV). This was the greatest transformation that ever occurred in my life, and I never wanted to go back. When you have a true born-again experience, you will never be the same nor will you want to be!

HOW WILL MY LIFE CHANGE ONCE I SURRENDER?

"Yet a time is coming and has now come when the true worshipers will worship the Father in the Spirit and in truth, for they are the kind of worshipers the Father seeks. God is spirit, and his worshipers must worship in the Spirit and in truth" (John 4:23-24 NIV).

From the moment you are spiritually "born again," you will notice a distinct difference in your life. This will be the beginning of your "new" life. When the Holy Spirit enters inside of you, you will become interested in the things of God! You will want to read the Bible, go to church, and listen more closely to the preacher. No one will have to force you, nor will you feel like it's your duty, because there is a force inside of you driving you in that direction. It's like a magnet with intensity drawing you closer to the things of God, and it's exciting! When you know that God is real, you will want more of God!

I remember the first non-denominational church I attended. I saw a man in the hallway with tattoos from head to toe. I wanted to go over to tell him how much Jesus loved him. This is when I really knew God did something on the inside of me because I never liked tattoos, nor would I have approached someone marred in them. My Bible reading also changed. It wasn't just stories that I could relate to, but it actually came alive; it was reading through a new lens! It had power that pierced the inside of me, and I couldn't get enough of it. I wanted to plaster the Word of God all over the walls of my home. I wanted everyone around me to know God was real, His Word and truth! This was just the beginning. The real permanent change would happen over time, one step at a time! The Lord prepared me beforehand and walked me through every difficulty, trial, persecution, tribulation, and suffering I would experience as I grew in my faith! This will be discussed in more depth in later chapters.

I AM A CHRISTIAN. DOESN'T THAT MEAN I HAVE ALREADY SURRENDERED?

"Oh, the joys of those who do not follow the advice of the wicked, or stand around with sinners, or join in with scoffers. But they delight in doing everything the Lord wants; day and night they think about his law" (Psalm 1:1-2 NLT). This scripture is a good basis for examining where you are in your spiritual walk of living a surrendered life.

Whose advice are you following? When it comes to getting advice for anything, you should go to the Father, Son, and Holy Spirit in prayer first. Read His Word as led by the Holy Spirit and seek out Christian mentors and accountability partners for direction and confirmation. Ultimately, wait on the Lord and the direction given by the Holy Spirit. As I've heard it said, "Go to the throne before the phone."

Standing around with sinners or joining in with scoffers would include establishing boundaries with those around you who are engaging in behaviors that are warned about in Scripture, such as gossiping, lying, cheating, stealing, and ridiculing others, just to name a few. "Let there be no sexual immorality, impurity, or greed among you. Such sins have no place among God's people. Obscene stories, foolish talk, and coarse jokes—these are not for you. Instead, let there be thankfulness to God" (Ephesians 5:3 NLT). Examine your own heart and behavior and what you are allowing to enter your life. I remember a few months after I was saved, watching a sexual movie with some friends, laughing at the scenes, and even relating to them and then thinking, "Should I be laughing at this? Should I even be watching this?" We watched the movie until the end, but as I grew in my faith, it became a thing of the past. If you find you are having difficulty turning from these behaviors, pray and ask the Holy Spirit to help you turn from them. "For I can do everything through Christ, who gives me the strength" (Phil 4:13 NLT).

Delighting in doing everything the Lord wants. Day and night they think about His law: You may say to yourself, "This is unrealistic, especially with a full-time job, being a student, or taking care of kids all day long." I would tell you that it is realistic. Praying and talking with God and His Word should be with you everywhere you go throughout your day. When things on the job, in the classroom, at home, or with the kids come up and you're not sure how to handle it, God knows exactly what you need to do. Praying and seeking His Word for direction and guidance from the Holy Spirit can happen any time of day, wherever you are. God wants to be included in every area of your life, and when you are surrendered, you will want to include the Lord. I remember my aunt who was discipling me in my early Christian walk over the phone. During our conversation, she would say, "Open your Bible," knowing it was right next to me.

If you don't have time to pray, read the Bible, and follow the leadership of the Holy Spirit, this would be an indication that you may not be as surrendered as you believe you are. Pray, repent, and ask the Holy Spirit to reveal to you what is preventing you from surrendering.

A REPENTANT LIFE IS A SURRENDERED LIFE!

God is waiting for you to surrender it all! This is the beginning of becoming a worshiper in Spirit and in truth! Pray according to Scripture, and ask God to make you this kind of worshiper! Your part is to repent, believe and surrender!

A prayer for surrender: Father God, I want to surrender all of my life to the lordship of Jesus Christ and the leadership of the Holy Spirit. Forgive me for doing it my way and not Your way. I humbly submit. I am not sure how, so please show me and help me to stay committed to Your plan for my life. I ask this in the name of Jesus, Amen.

Learning to follow the leadership of the Holy Spirit is critical to walking victoriously in your new surrendered life as we will discuss in the next chapter.

CHAPTER TWO

BE LED BY THE HOLY SPIRIT

THE HOLY SPIRIT will direct you to exactly where you need to go, what you need to do, and how to do it. God will lead you along your journey into His purpose for your life; all you have to do is follow. Your free will will never be violated, and the Holy Spirit's prompting will be in line with the Word and where you are on your spiritual journey. The Holy Spirit is your ultimate guide and only speaks to you what He hears from Jesus. As Scripture reveals: "However, when He, the Spirit of truth, has come, He will guide you into all truth; for He will not speak on His own authority, but whatever He hears He will speak; and He will tell you things to come. He will glorify Me, for He will take of what is Mine and declare it to you. All things the Father has are Mine. Therefore, I said that He will take of Mine and declare it to you" (John 16:13-15 NKJV). When we are following the voice of the Holy Spirit, we are following Jesus!

How do I live being led by the Holy Spirit? Pray, read the Scriptures, pray for revelation, and begin living your life on your job, in your family right where you are, where Jesus found you. The Scriptures confirm this: "You must accept whatever situation the Lord has put you in, and continue on as you were when God first called you"(1 Corinthians 7:17 NLT). On the day I got saved after receiving the visions, I went to my office and thought about what I should do next. I prayed and said, "Lord, what do I do now?" Staying connected to the Holy Spirit was critical for every step. I had a sense that veering off even slightly would be detrimental to my family's well-being. As spiritual warfare emerged, following closely to the prompting of the Holy Spirit guided me through situations that on my own, I would not have known which way to go to bring forth the best outcome.

When you are led by the Holy Spirit, He will guide you in areas to grow your faith. Where you should attend church, what scriptures you should memorize, to the worship music you should listen to. He will equip you with tools in your hands to move forward on your spiritual journey that is "unique" to only you. Just as God designed your own natural DNA, so it is with your spiritual DNA. Who knows your natural and spiritual DNA better than anyone, even more than yourself, your family, your pastor, or your doctor? The One who made you, the One who died for you, and the One who has been sent to guide you—the Father, Son, and the Holy Spirit. Be sensitive to the promptings and your internal knowledge when the Holy Spirit is talking to you and moving you along your journey.

TRUST THE HOLY SPIRIT EVEN WHEN IT DOESN'T MAKE SENSE.

"Trust in the Lord with all your heart; do not depend on your own understanding. Seek His will in all you do; and He will direct your paths" (Proverbs 3:5-6 NLT). This is a good scripture not just for memorizing but one to live by and reference over and over again, especially when circumstances become more challenging to your understanding. When situations arise that do not make sense to you, pray, lean on the Word, and trust the Holy Spirit is guiding you in the right direction.

In early 2006, my circumstances were becoming more hostile. At one point, I said, "I wish I had wings like a bird and could just fly away." Then on March 26, 2006, (I marked the date in my Bible), I was reading Psalm 55:

Oh, how I wish I had wings like a dove; then I would fly away and rest! I would fly far away to the quiet of the wilderness. It is not an enemy who taunts me—I could bear that. It is not my foes who so arrogantly insult me—I could have hidden from them. Instead, it is you my equal, my companion and close friend. What good fellowship we enjoyed as we walked together in the house of God. As for this friend of mine, he betrayed me; he broke his promises. His words are as smooth as cream, but in his heart is war. His words are as soothing as lotion, but underneath are daggers! Give your burdens to the Lord, and he will take care of you. He will not permit the godly to slip and fall. (Psalm 55:20-22)

I knew this was a description of what I was experiencing and wanted to flee But I had an inner sense, the Holy Spirit's prompting, that fleeing was not the answer. So, I prayed and waited on the Holy Spirit to give me the next step.

I continued down this path, and within a few months, a supplier demanded full payment on a negotiated settlement due to a missed payment. Within a couple of days, some people arrived with a court order unannounced and began changing the locks on the doors. Then they notified me they were shutting my company down and seizing all of my assets. I remember saying, "You've got to be kidding. We owe less than $10k, and my assets are worth hundreds of thousands of dollars. That didn't matter. They were enforcing the court order and taking everything they could put their hands on. This was a surreal experience! Even though it was happening, my mind was on what God was doing and what I was hearing from the Holy Spirit. I remained calm and cooperative. Finally, the leader of the agency pulled me aside and said, "I'm so sorry that I'm doing this to your company." Immediately, the Holy Spirit brought to my memory the scripture of Jesus before Pilate: "Then Jesus said, 'You would have no power over me at all unless it were given to you from above'" (John 19:11). So, I replied, "Don't be sorry. You're just doing your job. God is in control, and He'll bring me through."

This situation stopped all immediate revenue from my company and for the first time I stayed at home with my daughters and did what I could to salvage whatever was left of my business. I remember at this time the Lord gave me specific instructions on how to manage my schedule and planning. In a message I was reading, the Holy Spirit illuminated, "Don't try to fit Me (God) into your schedule; work your schedule around time with Me." Another message was: "Plan as if you're going to live a hundred years, but live each day as if it were your last." Then as I was reading in Matthew, Jesus said:

> Therefore, I tell you, do not worry about your life, what
> you will eat or drink; or about your body, what you will
> wear. Is not life more than food, and the body more than
> clothes? Look at the birds of the air; they do not sow or
> reap or store away in barns, and yet your heavenly Father

feeds them. Are you not much more valuable than they? Can anyone of you by worrying add a single hour to your life?

And why do you worry about clothes? See how the flowers of the field grow. They do not labor or spin. Yet I tell you that not even Solomon in all his splendor was dressed like one of these. If that is how God clothes the grass of the field which is here today and tomorrow is thrown into the fire, will he not much more clothe you—you of little faith? So do not worry, saying, "What shall we eat?" or "What shall we drink?" or "What shall we wear?" For the pagans run after all these things, and your heavenly Father knows that you need them.

But seek first His kingdom and His righteousness, and all these things will be given to you as well. (Matthew 6:25-33 NIV)

It was the last verse that really stood out to me, and I thought, "Alright Lord, I'm going to take You at Your Word! I'm going to do what You're saying, and the only way I know how to is to spend the majority of my time in Your Word, hearing Your Word, and learning and living Your Word!" I did this while I was taking care of my children and spending minimal time salvaging my business. I remember a Christian-owned business that had paid my company 10K to sell its services and called to find out how it was going. I shared with them that I believed the Lord wanted me to focus my time on being home and taking care of my family and less time on business. They were understanding and said, "You have to do what the Lord is telling you to do." This would come full circle in my life, as I will share in a later chapter.

ALLOW THE HOLY SPIRIT TO EXPOSE HIDDEN THINGS IN YOUR SOUL:

The Holy Spirit will bring to light deep hidden woundedness and lies in your personhood and psychological makeup as you yield to His leadership so that you can be free to be who God created you to be! What I'm about to share was the best-kept secret of my life. It wouldn't be until my late forties when the Lord would orchestrate events in my career that would open the "Pandora's box" to the deepest recesses of my soul. The secrets I was keeping were keeping me in spiritual bondage in my mind and emotions, from hidden trauma deep within my soul. "For there is nothing hidden which will not be revealed, nor has anything been kept secret but that it should come to light" (Mark 4:22 NKJV).

As an accomplished businesswoman, I found myself in a meeting being ridiculed and demoralized by a new leader in front of customers and colleagues. I was speechless and left the meeting driving in my car crying, wanting to submit my resignation. My initial instinct was to flee, but through the Holy Spirit, Word of God and godly counsel, I was being led how to properly handle and resolve this conflict and righteously stand for justice. This incident was the pandora's box to the little girl inside of me who was hiding childhood trauma of abandonment and abuse. It was a safeguarded secret throughout my life and my successful business lifestyle concealed it well. I had never spoken about the trauma from my childhood in detail until this incident occurred at age fifty, eleven years after my salvation. This brought to light what was really hiding and revealing it was freedom in my soul. While this may have been the best-kept secret in my life and the foundation in which my soul development was "derailed," rendering me "captive" in my emotions and relational areas, God had a plan! When I surrendered it all to the lordship of Jesus Christ and received the Holy Spirit, He began doing a work of unraveling and exposing the lies, deception, hurt, anger, rage, fear, and sin that permeated my being. The Holy Spirit began to "rebuild" my soul and create in me the woman of God I was called to be—loved!

"For God so loved the world that He gave his only begotten son that whosoever would believe in him would have eternal life" (John 3:16 NKJV). Although my heart longed for the love from others, my heavenly Father was preparing a way for me to receive His love!

I remember experiencing a disheartening situation. Realizing the anxiety I was feeling was excessive, I prayed and asked the Holy Spirit to reveal what was going on inside of me. "Search me, O God, and know my heart; test me and know my anxious thoughts. Point out anything in me that offends you, and lead me along the path of everlasting life" (Psalm 139:23-24 NLT). The Holy Spirit brought childhood memories to mind and with tears rolling down my face, I said, "Lord, all I ever wanted was for someone to come for me," and with a soft-spoken voice I heard clearly in my spirit, the Lord said, "Debra, I came for you!" It pierced my heart! I felt convicted and said, "I'm sorry Lord, I know you did. But help me to receive this! I just want to be able to hug you!"

There was another incident that had me internally enraged under severe mental and demonic oppression. After praying to the Holy Spirit to reveal what was going on, I was drawn to a Christian magazine article with a heading that read, "The Lord wants you to stop wanting your abuser punished!" I began to weep, realizing that was me, and my quest to seek justice was primarily driven by my deep internal desire to have my abuser punished. I repented, prayed, and asked the Holy Spirit to help me to overcome this. No matter what you've gone through God will receive you, as His Word acknowledges. "Though my father and mother forsake me, the Lord will receive me" (Psalm 27:10 NIV). In receiving the love of my heavenly Father, I could begin to forgive and love the people that hurt me beyond what was humanly possible. It didn't happen overnight; it was a process and a journey led by the Holy Spirit and only by the grace of God, even as of the writing of this book! Trauma, hurt, and pain that remain hidden will keep you in bondage. However, when you submit to the Holy Spirit's guidance, He will pinpoint exactly where you need inner healing, deliverance, and the way you personally need to be set free. Listen and respond to the Holy Spirit! "For nothing is secret that will not be revealed, nor anything hidden that will not be known and come to light" (Luke 8:17 NKJV). The Holy Spirit knows you best, and listening to His guidance will bring you through difficult situations victoriously! Learn to listen to the Holy Spirit!

LISTEN TO THE HOLY SPIRIT:

"Whether you turn to the right or to the left, your ears will hear a voice behind you saying, 'This is the way; walk in it'" (Isaiah 30:21 NIV).

"And when he brings out his own sheep, he goes before them; and the sheep follow him, for they know his voice. Yet they will by no means follow a stranger, but will flee from him, for they do not know the voice of strangers" (John 10:4 NKJV).

"My sheep listen to my voice; I know them and they follow me" (John 10:27 NLT).

When you receive the Holy Spirit, you will know His voice instinctually to be able to follow where He leads. Early on in my spiritual walk when things were really heating up, I asked the Lord to show me the difference between my thoughts, His thoughts, and the enemy's thoughts. I wanted to be able to distinguish clearly between them. Within 24 hours, the Lord revealed it to me. When it was my thought, I would be trying to figure something out, reasoning through a decision. When it was the Holy Spirit, it was a soft-spoken, peaceful prompting, and internal knowing. When it was the enemy, it was a condemning, gloomy, or destructive subtle thought that contradicted what I was learning in the Bible. This helped me to distinguish between the voices in my head as I was growing in my spiritual journey.

As you listen, the Holy Spirit will reveal the hidden things of God through revelation in Scripture. Revelation comes through the impartation of the Holy Spirit from the Word, preaching, prophetic teaching, or book. Whenever the Lord wants to impart knowledge, discernment, or wisdom in a particular area of your life, natural or supernatural, it is the Holy Spirit who imparts it to you. These impartations are not only used to bring knowledge but to separate you from the wisdom of the world to the wisdom of God.

But to those called by God to salvation, both Jews and Gentiles, Christ is the power of God and the wisdom of God. This foolish plan of God is wiser than the wisest of human plans, and God's weakness is stronger than the greatest of human strength. Remember, dear brothers and sisters, that few of you were wise in the world's eyes or powerful or wealthy when God called you. Instead, God chose things the world considers foolish in order to shame those who think they are wise. And he chose things that are powerless to shame those who are powerful. God chose things despised by the world, things counted as nothing at all, and used them to bring to nothing what the world considers important. As a result, no one can ever boast in the presence of God. (1 Corinthians 1:24-29 NLT)

There are messages just for you, spiritually imparted to your heart and mind to bring a clearer understanding of the Scriptures and how you should apply it to the specific situations you are facing. I remember a specific time comparing my talents and abilities which was bringing on warfare in my mind. After sharing my frustration with a believing friend, her advice was to listen to the Holy Spirit and "Go to the Word and find out, it's in there!" I really didn't like her answer because I wanted her to tell me exactly what she thought and where I should read in the Bible. But she did the right thing because it is the Holy Spirit who points you right where you need to go in the Word. As I was reading, the Holy Spirit led me to Philippians 2:3: "Do nothing out of selfish ambition or vain conceit. Rather in humility value others above yourselves, not looking to your own interests but each of you to the interest of others" (NIV). It caught my attention. Then I said, "Lord, is this me?" The Holy Spirit was bringing conviction that it was me. I knelt down, repented of selfish ambition, and asked God for forgiveness. Immediately, the spiritual warfare in my mind ceased, and at that moment, I was sanctified and separated from this sin!

When you're not sure what to do, just wait and listen for the Holy Spirit to direct you. He will meet you right where you are and communicate with you in a way that you will know. A good example is when you get an idea to do something or call someone, and when you do, you receive confirmation that your timing couldn't have been better. That is God's timing!

The Holy Spirit is your ultimate guide working to bring wholeness to your soul so that you can fulfill your purpose which God planned for you long before you ever showed up on this planet, for your generation today. It's important that as we are led by the Holy Spirit and He reveals things to us and actions we need to take, we do them and keep doing them! This is where not only being led by the Holy Spirit is needed, but once led, obedience is essential in your journey to be made whole and walk in your purpose, as we will discuss in the next chapter.

CHAPTER THREE

OBEDIENCE

OBEDIENCE IS A critical component to receiving what God has prepared for you on your path in life. Obedience will keep you from enduring unnecessary hardships and suffering and will bring you through trials and tribulations victoriously. "Study this Book of Instruction continually. Meditate on it day and night so you will be sure to obey everything written in it. Only then will you prosper and succeed in all you do" (Joshua 1:8 NLT). "Don't misunderstand why I have come. I did not come to abolish the law of Moses or the writings of the prophets. No, I came to accomplish their purpose" (Matthew 5:17 NLT).

Obedience is a precursor to tearing down idols and being sanctified, separating you from sin in your life such as pride, idolatry, deception, unbelief, and whatever else gets the majority of your attention that your mind is wired to. Obedience will come more naturally as you do it more and more.

When the Holy Spirit prompts you to do something, be obedient! That includes when He tells you not to do something. When you know that you know the Holy Spirit is speaking, don't hesitate to do exactly what He prompts you to do, nothing more and nothing less. "For I know the plans I have for you," declares the Lord, "plans to prosper you and not to harm you, plans to give you hope and a future" (Jeremiah 29:11-12 NIV).

The Holy Spirit had been impressing upon me for about a month to read the book of Daniel. At the same time, I had been asking the Lord, why did it take so long for me to surrender my life? On March 5, 2007, a little over a year after being saved, I received the answer.

As he looked out across the city, he said, "Just look at this great city of Babylon! I, by my own mighty power, have built this beautiful city as my royal residence and as an expression of my royal splendor. While he was still speaking these words, a voice called down from heaven. "O King Nebuchadnezzar, this message is for you! You are no longer ruler of this kingdom. You will be driven from human society. You will live in the fields with the wild animals, and you will eat grass like a cow. Seven periods of time will pass while you live this way, until you learn that the Most High rules over the kingdoms of the world and gives them to anyone he chooses." (Daniel 4:30-32 NLT)

"Now I, Nebuchadnezzar, praise and glorify and honor the King of heaven. All his acts are just and true, and he is able to humble those who are proud" (Daniel 4:37 NLT). It was humbling as the Holy Spirit was bringing conviction. I knew that was me. It was pride in my business and abilities. I repented and asked the Lord to forgive me. Then, I asked the Lord, "Is that what is going on? Have you sent me out to eat the grass?" I may not have eaten grass like Nebuchadnezzar but had already begun eating my share of humble pie, and there was more to come. Nevertheless, obedience to the Holy Spirit will ultimately prevail!

OBEDIENCE WILL CHALLENGE YOUR FLESH. DO IT ANYWAY.

"The Spirit is willing but the flesh is weak" is no understatement. It's the truth! Even when Jesus Himself asked His disciples to watch and pray, they couldn't do it.

Then Jesus came with them to a place called Gethsemane, and said to the disciples, "Sit here while I go and pray over there." And He took with Him Peter and the two sons of Zebedee, and He began to be sorrowful and deeply distressed. Then He said to them, "My soul is exceedingly sorrowful, even to death. Stay here and watch with Me." He went a little farther and fell on His face, and prayed, saying, "O My Father, if it is possible, let this cup pass from Me; nevertheless, not as I will, but as You will." Then He came to the disciples and found them sleeping, and said to Peter, "What! Could you not watch with Me one hour? Watch and pray, lest you enter into temptation. The Spirit indeed is willing, but the flesh is weak." (Matthew 26:36-40 NKJV)

Jesus asked the same thing of His disciples a second and third time, and again they fell asleep. It is very challenging to be a follower of Jesus; it goes against what our flesh wants to do, but the Holy Spirit was sent to empower us to "watch and pray"! We must stay awake!

Obedience will take your flesh places you weren't expecting to go or experience. It was my 40th birthday, and I thought to myself, "I sure didn't imagine this is where I would be at this time in my life." Here I was trying to settle into a home a quarter of the size of the home we moved out of and setting mouse traps to catch the unwanted visitors. Scripture says, "Everyone has heard about your obedience, so I rejoice because of you…" (Romans 16:19 NIV). While reading this, I was rather emotional, and said to myself, "What do you mean everyone knows about my obedience? No one knows what I'm going through." And then I had the thought,

"Oh, it's the people in heaven that are celebrating. Wonderful! But look where my obedience has gotten me." I was still very earthly-minded. I thought to myself, "I'm getting exactly what I deserve for the sinful life I lived," which in part was true; there is a consequence for the sin we engaged in before surrendering. As the tears were streaming down my eyes under a weight of guilt and condemnation, all of a sudden the sun started piercing through a very narrow window behind me. The entire room was illuminated so brightly that even my eyelashes were shining. I knew it was God and dropped to my knees in awe. His presence gave me reassurance that He was with me and I wasn't being punished. This brings tears to my eyes even today when I think about God meeting me there. It was a miraculous sign in my sight that encouraged me to continue on. It would not be the last time the Lord would visit me in this way throughout my journey. When you decide to be obedient, your flesh will not like it, but the Lord will encourage you along the way!

OBEDIENCE WILL BRING ON SPIRITUAL WARFARE. DO IT ANYWAY.

The enemy wakes up when you start getting serious about your walk with the Lord, which is usually when you make a decision to be obedient to where the Holy Spirit is leading. It is as if the enemy of our soul taunts us with questions like, "Are you sure this is the path you want to take? Is this really what you want to do? Can you handle the heat?" I didn't want to go back to the life I was living, and the only way out was through obedience to the Holy Spirit.

There is a spiritual battle going on every minute of every day, but Jesus has overcome the world, and you will have His peace, and the Holy Spirit and angels will war on your behalf. As Jesus said, "These things I have spoken to you, that in Me you may have peace. In the world you will have tribulation; but be of good cheer, I have overcome the world" (John 16:33 NKJV).

As my obedience was growing stronger, the spiritual warfare was revving up! We were down to one vehicle and the unthinkable happened. It was repossessed at the front door of the rental property we just moved into. When I noticed, panic started to arise within me, but then I thought, "Wait a minute, God is not shocked by what just happened. He sees the beginning from the end." For the Word of God says, "I make known the end from the beginning, from ancient times, what is still to come...My purpose will stand, and I will do all that I please" (Isaiah 46:10 NIV). He knew it was going to happen and prepared a way. I calmed down and prayed and asked the Lord what I should do. The Holy Spirit gave me direction.

The spiritual warfare and heightened threats both real and imagined brought fear into my heart about what was being done behind the scenes. I spent a lot of time crying out to God! Then, the Lord spoke these scriptures directly to me, "The Lord has said to me in the strongest terms: 'Do not think like everyone else does. Do not be afraid that some plan conceived behind closed doors will be the end of you. Do not fear anything except the Lord Almighty. He alone is the Holy One. If you fear him, you need fear nothing else'" (Isaiah 8:11-13 NLT).

I turned the pages over and read at the top of the page: "Every teacher of religious law who has become a disciple in the Kingdom of Heaven is like a person who brings out of the storehouse the new teachings as well as the old" (Matthew 13:52 NLT). I thought, "Oh my goodness, is this me, Lord, am I a disciple? Am I a teacher?" Internally, I felt a sense of safety that I had never experienced in my life, and when thoughts filled my mind that were contrary to only fearing God, I would stand against them and recite the scripture out loud again and again to my mind.

As the spiritual battles continued emerging, I would walk back and forth in my living room professing scriptures out loud. I would refute arguments and theories and reasonings and every proud and lofty thing that sets itself up against the knowledge of God and I led every thought and purpose away captive into the obedience of Christ (2 Corinthians 10:5 AMP). This was my Mayday call! I repeated it over and over and over again until the attacks in my mind would simmer down and go away. Surrendering to the Holy Spirit's guidance and the Word was the only way I got through this battlefield. It's the only way any of us will be able to get through. "For we do not wrestle against flesh and blood, but against principalities, against powers, against the rulers of the darkness of this age, against spiritual hosts of wickedness in the heavenly places" (Ephesians 6:12 NKJV). Whatever battle you may be going through, in your own disbelief that it is actually happening, you will come through it in obedience to the Holy Spirit and the Word! Your victory is on the other side of the battle, and your reward is transformation!

Obedience will bring transformation in your mind as you do it anyway. "Don't copy the behavior and customs of this world, but let God transform you into a new person by changing the way you think. Then you will know what God wants you to do, and you will know how good and pleasing and perfect His will really is" (Romans 12:2). Scripture is clear. We need to be transformed in our minds to know God's will for our lives. I needed "transformation" in my mind apart from spiritual deliverance. My own behavior needed to come into obedience.

There were behavioral patterns that had been developed over the years in my mind which needed to be transformed. When they were exposed and the Holy Spirit brought conviction, I immediately repented. I did this as often as needed, until there was a breakthrough, and the behavior was no longer an issue. This is a process and takes prayer, Holy Spirit intervention and perseverance. God doesn't give up on us, so never give up! Being confident of this very thing, that He who has begun a good work in you, will complete it until the day of Jesus Christ. (Philippians 1:6 NKJV).

It cannot be emphasized enough—repent, repent, repent! The Word, The Word, The Word! Obedience, obedience, obedience! The Word is Jesus and is alive with power! It's spiritual medicine and when taken into your soul with an open heart and mind and applied to your everyday life, you will be forever changed!

BE OBEDIENT TO THE WORD YOU HAVE RECEIVED.

"For the Word of God is alive and powerful. It is sharper than the sharpest two-edged sword, cutting between soul and spirit, between joint and marrow. It exposes our innermost thoughts and desires. Nothing in all creation is hidden from God. Everything is naked and exposed before his eyes, and he is the one to whom we are accountable" (Hebrews 4:12 NLT).

"But don't just listen to God's Word. You must do what it says. Otherwise, you are only fooling yourselves. For if you listen to the Word and don't obey, it is like glancing at your face in the mirror. You see yourself, walk away, and forget what you look like. But if you look carefully into the perfect law that sets you free, and if you do what it says and don't forget what you heard, then God will bless you for doing it" (James 1:22-25 NLT).

After receiving the word from the Lord in Matthew 13:52 about being a disciple and teacher, wondering if that was really about me, the Lord brought confirmation through the voice of a little boy.

While volunteering in my daughter's church preschool class, I heard from across the room a little boy calling out, like on a bullhorn, "Teacher, teacher." I wondered if he was calling me but dismissed it right away. Then he called again, "Teacher!" He was walking near me, and I asked him quietly what he had said. With a puzzled look on his face, he said, "Teacher." I said, "Oh, what do you need?" I sensed the Lord was speaking to me through this little boy that I was a teacher and kept it to myself.

It was interesting. A year after getting saved, church leaders wanted me to volunteer and become a small group leader, but I didn't feel equipped, so I declined. However, I signed up for the leadership classes. It is crucial to know the Word and apply it in your life for yourself. Where the Holy Spirit leads one person, may be different for another. You must rely on the Holy Spirit and the Word given to you to make your decisions, not on what a pastor, leader, or teacher is saying they did or what you should do. They are subject to error and do not have the final word for God in your life! The Holy Spirit may give someone a prophetic word of knowledge to speak over you, but even that you must test for yourself. "This will be the third time I am coming to you. By the mouth of two or three witnesses every word shall be established" (II Corinthians 13:1 NKJV). Whenever you have received a prophetic word, vision, or dream in line with God's Word and will, if it is from the Lord, it will always be confirmed no matter how long it takes. I have received confirmation about a ministry vision the Lord gave me early in my walk, even up to the writing of this book, 17 years later.

We always have a choice. That's what God gives us because we are not His robots. We can choose obedience or disobedience to the Lord's direction, and if we persist in disobedience, there is a consequence as revealed in the Word: "For all who have entered into God's rest have rested from their labors, just as God did after creating the world. So let us do our best to enter that rest. But if we disobey God, as the people of Israel did, we will fall" (Hebrews 4:10 NLT). Therefore do your best to be obedient and enter into His rest!

Here are a few good meditation scriptures. Let them become a part of you to help you in your walk of obedience to the Holy Spirit.

- Blessed are all who fear the Lord, who walk in obedience to Him. (Psalm 128:1 NIV)
- For those who are led by the Spirit of God are the children of God. (Romans 8:14 NIV)
- Your Word I have hidden in my heart, That I might not sin against You. (Psalm 119:11 NKJV)
- But He answered and said, "It is written, 'Man shall not live on bread alone, but by every Word that proceeds from the mouth of God.'" (Matthew 4:4 NKJV)

Additionally, listen to Christian anointed preaching, teaching, and worship music, and let the Holy Spirit help you in your walk of obedience. Keep in mind that "the gateway to life is very narrow and the road is difficult, and only a few ever find it" (Matthew 7:14 NLT).

There will be other seasons, which I refer to as "Quiet Times," where the spiritual warfare and surrounding circumstances are more subdued. This is no time to waste; it's preparation time, as we will discuss next.

CHAPTER FOUR
QUIET TIMES

THERE WILL BE seasons in your life when the noise surrounding you seems to simmer down; these are the "quiet times." These periods of calm will come and go and may last for a short or long period. It is a time to dig deeper in getting to know the God of the Bible, Jesus your Savior and Holy Spirit your guide, and to get the Word in you. It is a time to branch out and develop new spiritual relationships within the body of Christ. It's a time to learn more about your beliefs and faith, what it is and isn't as it relates to the truth of God's Word. Quiet times allow for soaking up the things of God so that when the noise returns, you are better equipped and more proactive rather than reactive when facing challenging situations, unexpected circumstances, tests, and temptations.

You need to know the Word for yourself and not leave it only to man's interpretation but to the Holy Spirit's revelation! I heard it said early on that God tells you all you need to know about all you need to know. Your job is to study and know His Word. It's in the quiet times that you have more time to immerse yourself in studying. The Bible wasn't written just for the people of its day but for us today to apply in every area of our lives. It is as relevant today as it was then!

Don't let the quiet times pass you by without utilizing your time wisely in reading and studying the things of God as you are led by the Holy Spirit. It is a time to be immersed, refreshed, renewed, and prepared for what is ahead of you.

IT'S A TIME TO BE IMMERSED:

"Be diligent to present yourself approved to God, a worker who does not need to be ashamed, rightly dividing the Word of Truth" (2 Timothy 2:15 NKJV). Every morning I would listen to the local preacher on the Christian radio station, and for several months he opened with the following scripture: "Do not remember the former things, nor consider the things of old. Behold I will do a new thing, now it shall spring forth; Shall you not know it. I will even make a way in the wilderness and rivers in the desert" (Isaiah 43:18 NKJV).

Immerse yourself in the new thing that God is doing, letting go of the old things that you knew so well! As you immerse yourself in the truth, the Lord will unravel the lies you believed in the past that are no longer relevant to your life. When you believe a lie, you will live a lie! But when the truth comes, the lie doesn't work anymore and has to be put behind you. During a quiet-time season, as my Bible reading was intensifying, going to Bible college became a consideration. I already had a Bachelor of Science degree in Business Administration with Marketing as a major and Advertising and Public Relations as a minor and didn't believe the Lord was opening the door for me to attend Bible College and really didn't want to go through intense study again. However, I remember sharing this with a believer, and he looked at all of the Christian books and Bibles on my dining room table and said, "What do you call this? This is intense study!" Unbeknownst to me, the Lord enrolled me in the University of the Holy Spirit, and if you have received the Holy Spirit, He will do the same for you! "But you have received the Holy Spirit, and he lives within you, so you don't need anyone to teach you what is true. For the Spirit teaches you all things, and what he teaches is true—it is not a lie. So, continue in what he has taught you, and continue to live in Christ" (1 John 2:27 NLT).

There are numerous lies we believe from our upbringing, religion, culture, and the people around us. As I was immersed in knowing God more, the time came for me to be water baptized. The non-denominational church I attended offered no classes on the subject, but there were many books written and the Bible had a lot to say about it. I wanted to know what the Bible had to say since I had believed for years that being baptized as a baby was my ticket to heaven. It was startling for me to realize that being saved and receiving the Holy Spirit kept me from hell and no other way. I needed confirmation about my religious upbringing theology. I thought, "Lord, if I had died the day before getting saved, would I have gone to hell even though I was baptized as a baby?" On a piece of paper with one line drawn down the middle, one side was saved today, and the other side was not saved yesterday. The answer to this question was important to me, and the quiet time allowed me to study religion, salvation, baptism, and getting to heaven.

In my studies and classes, the act of water baptism is preceded by repentance from sin and acknowledging Jesus as your Lord and Savior. Water baptism doesn't save; it is a proclamation of faith in Jesus that leads you to water baptism. It symbolizes that you have died to your old man and are rising to newness of life. I praised God for letting me live long enough to make that decision for myself. "I baptize with water those who turn from their sins and turn to God" (Matthew 3:11 NLT).

The Holy Spirit further lead me to study the early church in relationship to the church today. The similarities were uncanny. For my own experience, my religion was ideal as it provided a way for me to absolve myself of my sin, while believing that I was on my way to heaven. Works based church works for the flesh. It was alive and well in Bible times as it is in our times. But it does not save and will lead in the wrong direction. "Every plant not planted by my heavenly Father will be rooted up, so ignore them. They are blind guides leading the blind, and if one blind person guides another, they will both fall into the ditch" (Matthew 15:13-14 NLT). I got down on my knees, prayed, and thanked God that He brought me out from being blind! Just give me Jesus and the Bible. It may be your religious upbringing that the Lord wants to put behind you to embrace the new thing He has for you!

IT'S A TIME TO BE REFRESHED

It's a time of vitality and newness. It's a time when new revelations being revealed to you are so exciting and extraordinary. You can't wait to share it with someone and/or apply it to your life.

When you receive revelation, it's a knowledge that is spiritually imparted to your understanding into your heart and mind to see things from a godly and spiritual perspective, beyond your natural ability. I remember receiving revelation from listening to preaching on the following scriptures.

> You foolish Galatians! Who has bewitched you? Before your very eyes Jesus Christ was clearly portrayed as crucified. I would like to learn just one thing from you: Did you receive the Spirit by observing the law, or by

believing what you heard? Are you so foolish? After beginning with the Spirit, are you now trying to attain your goal by human effort? Have you suffered so much for nothing–if it really was for nothing? Does God give you his Spirit and work miracles among you because you observe the law, or because you believe what you heard? (Galatians 3:1-2 NLT)

The preacher preached that the early church had a way of slipping back into their old ways, and Paul was trying to remind them that the law is not the way to be right with God, but it's only through faith in Jesus. I thought, this is it, this is what happened. Just like ourselves, the first Christians were Jews and of course, we all tend to slip back into our old ways, so it makes sense that Christians at that time would slip back into the customs of the law that Judaism was built on. I was so excited to hear this! I looked around the church to see if there was anyone else as excited as I was. All I saw was bewilderment on the people's faces. I asked the Lord, "What's going on here? How come I'm getting it and they are not?" The Lord spoke in my Spirit and said, "Because I have you on O.B.T." (On the Bible Training)! I was just glad to know it!

One morning after dropping my daughters off at preschool, the teacher asked me if I was going to go to the Chapel, as parents were invited to join in. It wasn't in my plan to attend, but the Holy Spirit was drawing me to the Chapel. As they were singing and praising the Lord, they were raising their hands, which was never a part of my religious custom.

Religious flashback: One time in the church where I attended, the congregation was so moved by the singing of the choir that everyone clapped loudly and whistled, and the preacher admonished everyone and told us to stop, that this was to be solemn and we were acting in sin by getting loud! We all looked at each other like he was ridiculous, but no one dared to say anything to him because he was the leader.

Then the head of the school began her teaching. She was reading from the Old Testament, beginning in Joshua 2:1-4a:

Then Joshua, son of Nun, secretly sent two spies from Shittim, "Go, look over the land," he said, "especially Jericho." So, they went and entered the house of a prostitute, named Rahab and stayed there. The king of Jericho was told, "Look! Some of the Israelites have come here tonight to spy out the land." So, the King of Jericho sent this message to Rahab: "Bring out the men who came to you and entered your house, because they have come to spy out the whole land." But the woman had taken the two men and hidden them (NIV).

(Joshua 2:8-9 NIV): "Before the spies lay down for the night, she went up on the roof and said to them, "I know that the Lord has given this land to you and that great fear of you has fallen on us, so that all who live in this country are melting in fear because of you."

(Joshua 2:11-12,14 NIV): "When we heard of it, our hearts melted and everyone's courage failed because of you, for the Lord your God is God in heaven above and on the earth below. Now then, please swear to me by the Lord that you will show kindness to my family, because I have shown kindness to you. Give me a sure sign...'Our lives for your lives!' The men assured her. 'If you don't tell what we are doing, we will treat you kindly and faithfully when the Lord gives us the land.'"

(Joshua 6:1-5 NIV): "Now Jericho was tightly shut up because of the Israelites. No one went out and no one came in. Then the Lord said to Joshua, "See, I have delivered Jericho into your hands, along with its king and its fighting men. March around the city once with all the armed men. Do this for six days. Have seven priests carry trumpets of rams' horns in front of the ark. On the seventh day, march around the city seven times, with the priests blowing the trumpets. When you hear them sound a long blast on the trumpets, have all the people give a loud shout; then the wall of the city will collapse and the people will go up, every man straight in.""

(Joshua 6:22-24a NIV): "Joshua said to the two men who had spied out the land, 'Go into the prostitute's house and bring her out and all who belong to her, in accordance with your oath to her.' So, the young men who had done the spying went in and brought out Rahab, her father and mother and brothers and all who belonged to her. They brought out her entire family and put them in a place outside the camp of Israel. Then they burned the whole city down and everything in it."

At the end of reading these scriptures, she began her exhortation, paraphrasing to the best of my recollection; the people of Jericho thought the "walls" they were hiding behind were safe. Only Rahab had the courage to come out from behind those walls. And God is asking you today, what "walls" are you hiding behind, thinking you are safe? God says, "Come out! They are not safe! Only in Christ can you find safety!" When I heard these last words, I wanted to crawl down under the seats and cry like a baby. I said, "Lord, have I been doing it wrong all of these years?" It was at this moment the Holy Spirit separated my heart's loyalty from the religious lies I believed.

> (Isaiah 44:20 NLT): "The poor, deluded fool feeds on ashes. He is trusting something that can give him no help at all. Yet he cannot bring himself to ask, 'Is this thing, this idol that I'm holding in my hand, a lie?'"

With tears in my eyes, I raised my hands for the first time and began worshiping the Lord as I had never before and have since continued. This was a spiritual work of sanctification by the Holy Spirit during a time of refreshing.

IT'S A TIME TO BE RENEWED

"In its place you have clothed yourselves with a brand-new nature that is continually being renewed as you learn more and more about Christ, who created this new nature in you" (Colossians 3:10 NLT). What is this new nature that Christ has created in you?

"Since God chose you to be the holy people whom He loves, you must clothe yourselves with tenderhearted mercy, kindness, humility, gentleness, and patience. You must make allowance for each other's faults and forgive the person who offends you. Remember, the Lord forgave you, so you must forgive others. And the most important piece of clothing you must wear is love. Love is what binds us all together in perfect harmony" (Colossians 3:12-14 NLT).

When my oldest daughter was in second grade in a religious school and my youngest daughters were in a Bible based Christian school, I began to contemplate transferring my oldest to the Christian school. But I still wasn't certain. I kept praying and thinking that they have to be teaching something right. They have the Bible, and they profess Jesus, so what is it that is not right? After much prayer, the Lord would begin to orchestrate circumstances that would reveal the motives, theology, and what they were teaching in the religious school. Almost as a spiritual encounter, I watched teachers gossip with one another about the kids, rather than lifting the kids up and helping them to come out of wrong behavior. They were labeling and accusing them and even shared it with me. I began to see the difference for myself between a Bible-based school and a religious-based school. Yet I still wasn't absolutely certain that moving my daughter was the right decision. So again, I prayed and read Scripture until I received confirmation from the Lord that this was the right move. It took about six months of deliberating this decision and finally, events would line up. And every time I would have an encounter at the religious school, the following scripture would be brought to my mind: "These people honor me with their lips, but their hearts are far from me. Their worship is a farce, for they replace God's commands with their own man-made teaching" (Matthew 15:8-9 NLT).

At the same time, we were attending a non-denominational Bible based church at the 10:00 am service and a religious service at noon. However, through the work of the Holy Spirit, Bible reading, and continued attendance between the two different services, it was becoming clear that we needed to break free from attending the religious service. On May 8, 2007, the following scripture in Isaiah was illuminated as if on a billboard, blinking on and off: "And so the Lord says, 'These people say they are mine. They honor me with their lips, but their hearts are far away. And their worship of me amounts to nothing more than human laws learned by rote (Isaiah 29:13 NLT, emphasis added). The definition of "rote" is the use of memory, usually with little intelligence. Routine or repetition carried out mechanically or unthinkingly. This would sum up my thirty-plus years of experience in a religious Church. There was no thinking required; it was routine. In fact, I thought since I could remember the words spoken by the leader on Sunday and the congregation's response, I had a front-row seat in heaven. I couldn't have been further from the truth! It was the blind being led by the blind, both falling into a ditch. This was enough to decide to stop attending the second service on Sundays at the religious church and transfer my oldest daughter to the Bible based Christian school.

When you are renewed through the Word and guided by the Holy Spirit, you can make life-long decisions in line with the Gospel of Jesus Christ that will enable you to live in truth, not from a religious or man-made perspective! You will be renewed from glory to glory! "But we all, with unveiled face, beholding as in a mirror the glory of the Lord, are being transformed into the same image from glory to glory, just as by the Spirit of the Lord" (2 Corinthians 3:18 NKJV).

Quiet times are preparation times for your continued Christian journey. As His children, the Lord wants to prepare us for what lies ahead, so we must do our part. Be sensitive to where the Holy Spirit directs. Sign up for the Bible Study, listen to the extra teaching, buy the worship song, watch a prophetic ministry or preacher, and pray more! At the beginning of 2020, the Holy Spirit revealed to me it was time to get back into writing my book. Then Covid19 hit, the world was shut down, and my attention was derailed from book writing. By summer, the Lord sent a prophetic word that put me back on track, and He will do the same for you! Stay the course so that when testing and trials come, you will stand strong. Emerging from the quiet times can bring on tests of faith, which we will delve into next.

CHAPTER FIVE

FAITH TESTS

L ET'S TALK ABOUT faith! What is faith? Where do we get it? How much do we need? What do we do with it? The Bible answers all these questions.

"Now Faith is the substance of things hoped for, the evidence of things not seen" (Hebrews 11:1 KJV).

"So, you see, it is impossible to please God without faith. Anyone who wants to come to him must believe that there is a God and that He rewards those who sincerely seek him" (Hebrews 11:6 NLT).

"So, then faith comes by hearing, and hearing by the Word of God" (Romans 10:17 NKJV).

"You didn't have enough faith," Jesus told them. "I assure you, even if you had faith as small as a mustard seed you could say to this mountain, 'Move from here to there,' and it would move. Nothing would be impossible" (Matthew 17:20 NLT).

"Do not merely listen to the Word, and so deceive yourselves. Do what it says...In the same way, faith by itself, if it is not accompanied by action, is dead"(James 1:22; 2:17 NIV).

According to the Scriptures, we do not see faith. It is the evidence of the things we cannot see, but hope for. We cannot please God or receive from Him without faith. Faith comes by hearing the Word of God. We hear the Word of God anytime we are listening to the Scriptures being spoken and in our reading out loud to ourselves. The evidence of our faith is whether we are doing what it says for us to do. So, we can reasonably deduce that our actions in doing what the Word tells us to do are an indicator of our faith.

The Bible is clear that apart from the Lord (The Word), we can do nothing: "Yes, I am the vine; you are the branches. Those who remain in me, and I in them, will produce much fruit. For apart from me you can do nothing" (John 15:5 NLT).

God tests our faith to reveal our level of faith to us, not to Him. How do we know we have anything unless it is tried and tested? Faith tests prove our faith. God will give you multiple opportunities to pass your test. You cannot fail; you will always get a redo. Faith tests expose the fruit of the Spirit developing within us. There will be circumstances that arise on the job, with your spouse, children, other believers, leaders, church, and everywhere you are planted, that will require exercising the fruit of the Spirit in line with the scripture you are studying. This is the ground for faith tests. They will be ongoing throughout our Christian walk and with each passing test, our faith will be strengthened and empower us to stay the course. It is usually when we get to the other side of the test that we realize how much our faith has grown.

Faith tests come in various ways; we will explore four types: belief tests, waiting tests, trust tests, and love tests.

BELIEF TESTS:

Belief tests test the level of what you believe about God and His Word, especially during grim circumstances. Will you still believe that God has a good plan for your life even though all hell may be breaking out? Your heart is breaking; your mind is going crazy; the people around you are repelling you, but God says, "Praise Me anyway." Really? Yes! It works. Put your faith to work!

God reveals to us that it is His Spirit and Word that give us life and life to believe.

> "It is the Spirit who gives life; the flesh profits nothing. The words that I speak to you are Spirit, and they are life" (John 6:63 NLT).

Our personal testimony is our reassurance to believe in the Father, Jesus, and the Holy Spirit. When we are walking through belief tests, we can rely on our testimony of God's revelation in our life when doubt arises. "I am [Jesus] praying not only for these disciples, but also for all who will ever believe in me because of their testimony" (John 17:20 NLT). Furthermore, the Word says that God is looking for those who will worship Him in Spirit and in truth! "But the hour is coming, and now is, when the true worshipers will worship the Father in Spirit and truth; for the Father is seeking such to worship Him" (John 4:23 NKJV). We can only worship in Spirit and in truth when we believe!

Before my faith was tested, God prepared me during the quiet times and previous faith tests for the next tests. That is good news!

We would rather not have to go through the test, but it is in the test that our faith grows and draws us closer to the Holy Spirit and what the Lord has prepared for us. You can compare it to going to school. In order to move from one grade to another, you have to take tests to ensure that you are ready to move on to the next grade. With the higher grade level come new tests, similar to your spiritual growth!

I remember praying and asking the Lord to help me to be proactive rather than reactive during tough times. My prayer was to be able to stand strong in faith when bad situations or trouble would arise rather than crying out to God in helpless desperation. The Lord answered my prayer, and the Holy Spirit walked me through a circumstance founded on a scripture that would be the springboard to prepare and alert me in future occurrences.

I was sitting alone in my car in an empty parking lot, eating lunch, listening to Christian music, and contemplating a difficult situation. Crying out to God, with tears streaming down my eyes, I said, "Lord, do you see what is happening? There is no way this can turn out well." The Holy Spirit brought this scripture to my mind: "Give thanks in all circumstances; for this is God's will for you in Christ Jesus" (1 Thess. 5:18 NIV).

Then the Lord spoke within my Spirit and said, "Raise your hands, Debra, and praise Me!" My reply was, "Lord, I don't want to praise You for this, but I will because Your Word says so!" As my arms were rising in worship to the Lord, a deep cry came out from within me which I never experienced before. I had a sense that God was healing me from something, deep inside, but I didn't know what. This was a transformational experience and afterward, the circumstance did not carry as much weight. Although it did not look good in the natural, it was at that moment I realized that what may not look good from a natural perspective can be good spiritually. It also made it easier for me to accept and push through, knowing that it was God's will. So, I didn't have to second-guess my own actions, or someone else's, or put it on the devil; it was God! What a relief. When we act on the Word of God and the prompting of the Holy Spirit, even when something bad is happening from our perception and cognitive ability, God can and will work it out for our good and grow our faith to believe! "And we know that God causes everything to work together for the good of those who love God and are called according to His purpose for them" (Romans 8:28 NIV).

Another situation occurred after being a more seasoned believer. I was walking into my office early one morning, and the Holy Spirit spoke to my spirit: "Give thanks in all circumstances; for this is God's will for you in Christ Jesus" (1 Thess. 5:18 NIV). I was startled. I thought, "Oh, no, what could it be?" So many things were going through my head. I had been working for a global automotive manufacturing company in a lead role with much success.

However, a year prior, I filed a complaint with human resources over the unprofessional behavior of a new vice president. My allegations were supported by a witness; however, this did not go well in the eyes of his colleague, a senior vice president. I remember as he walked by my office, his eyes said that if he could get rid of me that day, he would. I felt fear but counteracted it by knowing that God brought me there and would move me in His timing.

This was almost to the day a year later. I sat at my desk, prayed, and asked the Holy Spirit what I should do. I heard clearly in my spirit, "Do your job." So, I did. Just after lunch, a director came to my office and asked me to walk with him to the Human Resources department. They informed me that my position with the company was being terminated due to reorganization and offered various severance package options. As they were talking, I was thinking, "Wow, Lord, this is unbelievable. Thank You for preparing me!" They asked me what I wanted to do, and I responded, "Well, this is all just happening. I'll need time to think about it." They followed me back to my office with boxes to move me out, watching my every move. I reassured them that I would leave everything in order so that they could proceed with their business. As the director walked me to my car with a baffled look on his face, his last words to me were, "I just have to ask, HOW ARE YOU HANDLING THIS SO WELL?" Recognizing this as a witnessing opportunity, I shared my faith and said, "I'm not sure if you are aware of this, but I am a Christian and a follower of Jesus Christ. I believe whatever door He closes, He will open another door for me to walk through. So, my faith is in God alone and because of that, I'm thankful for the time I had at this company and can walk away in peace and wish you all the best moving forward."

> "The steps of a [good and righteous] man are directed and established by the Lord, And He delights in his way [and blesses his path]" (Psalm 27:23 AMP).

So, no matter what you are going through, by faith, believe the Lord is ordering your steps and follow the leadership of the Holy Spirit! The Holy Spirit will give you the next step; you just have to wait for it! This leads us to the waiting tests.

WAITING TESTS:

How long, Lord? It is difficult for our flesh to wait on the Holy Spirit to give the next step and confirmation. "By the mouth of two or three witnesses every word shall be established" (2 Corinthians 13:1b NKJV). But it is essential! It can be the difference between spiritual success or setback, healing, or further wounding. "But those who wait on the Lord Shall renew their strength: They shall mount up with wings like eagles, They shall run and not be weary, They shall walk and not faint" (Isaiah 40:31 NKJV)

When you are waiting, it can seem like forever, but it is just a season, a moment in time. It can be especially challenging when you know how to handle a situation, but the Holy Spirit prompts you to do nothing except wait. Or when you see something ahead and you want to do something but the Lord confirms, "Not by might, nor by power, but by My Spirit" (Zechariah 4:6 NKJV). Waiting is an amazing posture both in the natural and supernatural realms!

Your ability to wait reveals your level of patience and your fear of the Lord versus your fear of man or the enemy. As the famous words of the song, "Amazing Grace," go, "Twas grace that taught my heart to fear and grace my fears relieved, how precious was that grace appeared the hour I first believed." "Work out your salvation with fear and trembling; for it is God who works in you both to will and to do for His good pleasure" (Philippians 2:12b NKJV). It can become quite challenging when you are in the middle of a difficult circumstance to stand your ground in what God has called you to do, especially when family, friends, and even other believers are advising you otherwise. This is when your waiting test has the best potential to move you away from the fear of man to the fear of God. "Do not be afraid of those who want to kill you. They can only kill your body; but they cannot touch your soul. Fear only God, who can destroy both soul and body in hell" (Matthew 10:28 NLT). The fear of the Lord builds over time as we go through various tests, and God always proves Himself faithful, even when we are not, and He shows up in ways that can only be explained as the hand of God! The awesome fear of God is both a reverential fear and a realization that God can do whatever He wants to do but always has man's best interest in mind for eternal purposes!

"But our God is in heaven; He does whatever He pleases" (Psalm 115:3 NKJV).

Waiting also develops patience and brings about perfection and completeness in us. How do we know if patience has had its perfect work in our lives? "My brethren, count it all joy when you fall into various trials, knowing that the testing of your faith produces patience. But let patience have its perfect work, that you may be perfect and complete, lacking nothing" (James 1:2-4 NKJV).

One way we know when we have grown in our level of patience is when tests that previously brought on high levels of anxiety within us are now minimal to non-existent with no adverse effects on our minds and bodies. This is a work in progress until Jesus returns or calls us home. However, no matter how many times you have to go through the waiting test, never give up as the Holy Spirit leads and/or course corrects.

Waiting builds trust in the Lord and His provision to make the crooked paths straight. "I will go before you and make the crooked places straight; I will break in pieces the gates of bronze and cut the bars of iron. I will give you the treasures of darkness and hidden riches of secret places, That you may know that I, the Lord, Who call you by your name, Am the God of Israel" (Isaiah 45:2-3 NKJV).

Trust is a key component in all relationships and so it is with our relationship with the Father, Son, and Holy Spirit. Waiting and trusting in the Lord go hand in hand, which leads us to trust tests.

TRUST TESTS:

Do we really trust God? Can God trust us? These are two key questions and "trust tests" expose our level of trust. "The eyes of the Lord search the whole earth in order to strengthen those whose hearts are fully committed to him" (2 Chronicles 16:9a NLT).

Are you trusting in yourself, your money, talents, man, or in God, His Word, Jesus, and the Holy Spirit? This is the question you must ask yourself during times of testing because when we put our trust in anything but God alone, we are setting ourselves up for disappointment and deception, whether we know it or not.

Trusting God has to go beyond how we see things and how we believe it should have worked out. Trust that His ways are higher and His thoughts are different from ours: "My thoughts are completely different from yours," says the Lord. "And my ways are far beyond anything you could imagine. For just as the heavens are higher than the earth, so are my ways higher than your ways and my thoughts higher than your thoughts" (Isaiah 55:8-9 NLT). Trust that even when we are questioning if we missed it or failed in some way, God can still work it out for our good. "And we know that God causes everything to work together for the good of those who love God and are called according to His purpose for them" (Romans 8:28 NIV).

Are you trusting yourself or God? Putting your complete trust in God is not as easy as it sounds from a natural perspective. I learned through my studies that trust or the lack of trust is molded into our developing souls (minds). We either learn to trust or not, by how we are loved, protected, and provided for by our parents or caregivers during our most vulnerable stages of life, (womb through early childhood). Bonding and attachment fostered during these early stages play a significant role later in life in navigating life's challenges and relationships. When we have been wounded through trauma, (rejection, neglect, abuse), trusting can be life-threatening. Our mind was designed by God with a built-in protective mechanism that operates on chemical impulses and stores trauma in our unconscious mind when we are unable to process it. When future events mirror the same chemical releases, our mind kicks into the established protective mechanisms, forcing our reaction as originally programmed, usually by either a fight or flight response with heightened levels of anxiety. A key indicator of whether or not we are trusting and relying on God can be assessed by our level of anxiety. I remember when the Holy Spirit guided me to this scripture:

> "Stop putting your trust in mere humans. They are as frail as breath. How can they be of help to anyone?" (Isaiah 2:22 NLT).

I thought, "Wow, this is so true! No worries, Lord, I don't trust anyone anyway! This will be an easy scripture for me to follow wholeheartedly." Then the Holy Spirit spoke in my heart, "That includes you, Debra. You have to stop trusting in yourself!" This was a shock to my internal nervous system! My mind's programming, established during childhood, was that those in authority over me could not be trusted. So, if I could not trust the authority figures in my life, how could I trust God? The answer was, I could not. Because even God didn't stop it from happening. This became so deeply ingrained in my mind that trusting solely in my values and beliefs took precedence in every area of my life. But God was working to bring me to complete trust in Him. When the Holy Spirit brought conviction with this Word, I was humbled and my response was, "Okay, Lord, but You're going to have to help me because I do not know how to trust in anyone but myself." Only God's Word and the Holy Spirit have the power to break through our mind's protective programming and defense mechanisms, no matter how deep it goes.

"For the Word of God is alive and powerful. It is sharper than the sharpest two-edged sword, cutting between soul and spirit, between joint and marrow. It exposes our innermost thoughts and desires" (Hebrews 4:12 NLT).

I believe it was for this very reason the Holy Spirit guided me to research and study how our mind develops from a neurological and psychological perspective and how to be transformed and delivered from a theological perspective with the Holy Spirit's leading and God's Word! "And if the light you think you have is actually darkness, how deep that darkness is!" (Matthew 6:23b NLT).

I learned how God designed our minds with three levels: the conscious, the subconscious, and the unconscious. Our mind will automatically hide trauma in the unconscious realm as a protective mechanism against events that our undeveloped soul cannot process; the "proverbial" light came on for me! For years I questioned and was angry with God for allowing me to go through the things I did in my childhood. I could not wrap my mind around how God could just sit back and watch me being abused as a child and not do something about it. Yet the preacher said, "Forgive as God forgives you. Jesus suffered a sinner's death so that you could be set free." In my mind, I thought, "Yes, Jesus did suffer, but He was in His thirties when He went to the cross!" I would say, "Where were you God, when I was being abused as a little child?" The church's answer was that God doesn't interfere with our free will, and we should forgive those who hurt us, and God will do the healing. That wasn't enough for me. I needed more of an understanding. When I read in Isaiah that God was willing to reason with us, I was glad because that's what I needed. "Come now, and let us reason together," Says the Lord, "Though your sins are like scarlet, They shall be as white as snow; Though they are red like crimson, They shall be as wool" (Isaiah 1:18).

God revealed to me that He did do something about it before it ever happened. He created the human mind for survival, to survive through traumatic experiences even apart from living for Him, and to be revived at the cross through His Word and Spirit! This was humbling! We are born first to survive, then reborn to thrive!

> "Do not be conformed to the pattern of this world, but be transformed by the renewing of your mind" (Romans 12:2a NIV).

> "And even now the ax is laid to the root of the trees. Therefore, every tree which does not bear good fruit is cut down and thrown into the fire" (Matthew 3:10 NKJV).

This knowledge fueled my desire to dig deeper into the Word and rely more on the Holy Spirit. The more I studied, memorized, and applied Scripture in every area of my life, the stronger I grew in my faith and trust in the Holy Spirit. The more I applied truth, the more my thinking and behavior changed from the inside out. The Word and Spirit were permeating my being as I was beginning to rise up in the truths of the Gospel, that God loved me and that was enough! Even though I didn't love myself or felt as if anyone apart from my children had ever really loved me. This brings us to the next most important test, the love test.

LOVE TESTS:

Are you walking in love with God and people? I believe the greatest test is the love test. Why? Because God is Love!

> "And you shall love the Lord your God with all your heart, with all your soul, with all your mind and with all your strength. This is the first commandment. And the second, like it, is this: 'You shall love your neighbor as

yourself.' There is no greater commandment than these" (Mark 12:30-31 NKJV).

When your faith is put to the love test, you find out if you are loving God and others according to the Word. "Now by this we know that we know Him, if we keep His commandments. He who says, 'I know Him,' but does not keep His commandments, is a liar, and the truth is not in him. But whoever keeps His Word, truly the love of God is perfected in him. By this we know that we are in Him" (1 John 2:3-5 NKJV).

FAITH TAKES US ON A LOVE WALK.

- Loving God. To love God is to know His love for you. "We love Him because He first loved us" (1 John 4:19 NKJV). When you see yourself in light of the Gospel of Jesus Christ, it will bring you to your knees in gratitude for the love of God that saved you! It is His love that sent Jesus to the cross. His love that made a way when there was no way. His love that encourages us to keep going no matter what. His love that gives us grace and mercy to enter into His presence. When we really get a revelation of this, loving God overflows from a heart filled with love!

Knowing the Father's love reaches deep inside of us to reveal our true character and integrity, which is best observed during two opposing situations in our lives.

- When we are getting what we want.
and
- When we are not getting what we want.

When we are getting what we want, are we receiving it with humility and thankfulness to the Lord? Are we giving back, or are we hiding or holding on to it? When we are not getting what we want, is our response still praising the Lord, or are we exhibiting anger, bitterness, envy, and jealousy?

The Lord will engineer circumstances in your life to reveal what is really in your heart so that you know. When these situations arise, take a heart consideration check and ask the Holy Spirit to reveal to you what you cannot see. When you know how much God loves you, your behavior will be that of thankfulness when you are getting what you want and when you are not.

In the first few years of being saved, I listened intently to a well-known encouraging television preacher regularly, who said, "It doesn't matter what you've done. God loves you, and He has great plans for your life." I needed to hear this, to know that God loved me. Because most of my life had been lived without love, and I couldn't believe God could love me because of the sins I committed and the shame I was entangled with by my mere existence. Before surrendering my life to Jesus, the last thing I would have ever wanted was for anyone to benefit from my pain and suffering. In fact, my desire was that everyone would suffer. That was the condition of my heart. Even so, God allowed me to bring into the world my first daughter at age 32. It opened my heart to love in ways I could never have imagined. I couldn't thank God enough for sending me a little girl, and He not only blessed me with one daughter, but four years later with twin daughters. The love that I had for them was beyond words and nothing that I achieved or held in high esteem compared. It was this love that began drawing me closer to the Lord. Thank God that he doesn't hold our sins against us and blesses us anyway. "Children are a gift from the Lord…" (Psalm 127:3a NLT).

The greatest display of love was paying our sin debt at the cross! As I began to accept God's love as real, I expected that my surrounding circumstances and relationships would flourish, but that was not my reality. In fact, as I grew more in my faith, the world around me was getting uglier, and more and more demonic attacks were happening. I thought, "Is there something I'm missing?" The next several years would uncover hidden lies, motives, and agendas that would grow my faith and lead me into a closer relationship with the Holy Spirit while I was learning to love people, especially the ones that were hardest to love.

- Loving others. To love others is to love God. However, loving God can be a lot easier than loving people, with the God we make up in our minds, but the Word is clear you show your love for God by loving others.

"No one has ever seen God; but if we love one another, God lives in us and his love is made complete in us" (1 John 4:12 NIV).

The barometer to test how you are loving others can be measured by your level of forgiveness. Forgiveness and love go hand in hand. Forgiveness includes everyone, including yourself. Love and forgiveness take time, effort, and work. It involves setting godly boundaries around yourself as well as in your relationships. If you are loving someone out of fear of losing the relationship, this may be an indication that you are not in a godly relationship but one fueled by the enemy. You may have to separate yourself from relationships that are damaging and destructive to your personhood and your commitment to following Jesus in order for your heart to heal and love. You can forgive and love someone from a distance if the relationship is toxic to your soul, including within marriage. It may not be easy, but with the help of the Holy Spirit, it is possible. Allow the Holy Spirit to direct you in these areas. He knows what is best for you! Loving relationships are God-honoring! There may be times that you are in a difficult relationship, but God has you there for Kingdom purposes. When I found myself in these kinds of relationships, I would pray, "Lord, if there is no Kingdom purpose, please close the door and throw away the key, but if there is Kingdom purpose, please give me the grace to walk through it." Or with a difficult person, "God change him/her or remove him/her." You have to assess in your life whether you are affecting them for good or they are infecting you with their sin. God will answer your prayer and give you direction in line with His will for your life, in Jesus' name!

> "Owe no man anything but to love one another, for he that loveth another hath fulfilled the law" (Romans 13:8 KJV).

I've heard it said, "When we are walking in love, it is kryptonite to the enemy!"

> "Love has been perfected among us in this: that we may have boldness in the day of judgment; because as He is, so are we in this world. There is no fear in love: but perfect love casts out fear. But he who fears has not been made perfect in love" (1 John 4:17-18 NKJV).

Faith working in love cancels fear and brings us through tests victoriously. It is the critical component for living a victorious life in Christ! It gives us victory over demonic attacks and frees us from condemnation to live out our salvation.

> "There is therefore now no condemnation to those who are in Christ Jesus, who do not walk according to the flesh, but according to the Spirit" (Romans 8:1 NKJV).

Let this scripture pour over every part of your being, heart, mind, will, emotions, body, soul, and spirit. Receive it through God's love, grace, and mercy exemplified at the cross of Jesus Christ. This is where true freedom is found, as we will explore next.

CHAPTER SIX

TRUE FREEDOM

WHAT IS TRUE freedom? True "freedom" comes from within! Inward freedom means overflowing with the joy of the Lord regardless of the circumstances. It's the confidence of knowing that you know that God's got you! It's not freedom from the outside; it's freedom from the inside out! You can be in jail or anywhere in the world and still have this freedom.

> "For the law of the Spirit of life in Christ Jesus has made me free from the law of sin and death" (Romans 8:2 NKJV).

Jesus said to the people who believed in Him, "You are truly my disciples if you remain faithful to my teachings. And you will know the truth and the truth will set you free" (John 8:31-32 NLT). "So if the Son sets you free, you will be free indeed" (John 8:36 NIV).

True freedom is the gift of peace that comes from the Lord, which permeates your being regardless of your circumstances and only comes from Jesus.

"I am leaving you with a gift—peace of mind and heart. And the peace I give isn't like the peace the world gives. So don't be troubled or afraid" (John 14:27 NLT, emphasis added).

You can experience true freedom from mental and spiritual strongholds (overcoming your flesh, the world, and the enemy) when you surrender completely to the lordship of Jesus Christ and allow the Holy Spirit to lead you step by step. It was for this reason that Jesus came into the world as first told in Isaiah 61:1 and reiterated when He preached His first sermon in the gospel of Luke: "The Spirit of the Lord is upon Me, Because the Lord has anointed Me To preach the gospel to the poor; He has sent me to heal the brokenhearted, To proclaim liberty to the captives, And recovery of sight to the blind, To set at liberty those who are oppressed" (Luke 4:18 NKJV).

FREEDOM IN YOUR MIND:

Our mind is a vast and great machine that keeps us functioning in less-than-ideal environments and situations. We were designed this way by God to survive in a fallen sinful world, with an innately sinful nature. As touched upon in the previous chapter, our mind retains every memory and experience from our mother's womb throughout our lifespan. Our values, beliefs, thought patterns, memories, and habits become embedded in our minds (flesh) from early childhood. Trauma and negative words spoken become encapsulated and protected in the subconscious, as well as repressed memories and forbidden behaviors in the unconscious mind, which become a breeding ground for demonic oppression, possession, and infiltration. Trauma also affects our mind neurologically, through the release and withholding of chemicals which our mind uses to communicate between neurons to perform various functions. The mental health community will prescribe drugs to regulate a person's brain/mind chemicals for behavior modification. The Word of God has the power to rewire a person's mind around trauma, restart the brain's maturation process through the proper release of chemicals (serotonin, dopamine, norepinephrine, adrenaline) and transform behavior to a godly worldview. (You can learn more about soul/mind development in my Bible study book, Discovering Your Spiritual DNA).

The Holy Spirit can take you right to where you need deliverance and healing from strongholds in your mind and flesh. No one in the world, including yourself, has this ability; only the Lord knows exactly when it happened, how it happened, and where it happened. Ask the Holy Spirit to reveal to you where you need healing and deliverance in your mind. I'll share some of my experiences where the Holy Spirit led me in this area. God knows everything about us, our sitting down and our rising up, as written, "O Lord, you have examined my heart and know everything about me. You know when I sit down or stand up. You know my every thought when far away" (Psalm 139:1-2 NLT).

I learned through researching soul development that attachment problems are adaptations on the part of an infant/child for survival and self-protection. A typical personality trait for a child with an attachment problem is "control." The child will do whatever it takes to control every aspect of their environment. They experience control as comfort and security. When the parent or caregiver was in control, they initially experienced anxiety and fear.

Relinquishing control of every aspect of my life to the lordship of Jesus Christ was very difficult. It required complete reliance on the Holy Spirit, hearing the Word, believing the Word, and acting upon the Word. It was then my mind could begin being set free from the captivity of lies and deception that were intricately woven into my developing soul.

"Yes, I am the vine; you are the branches. Those who remain in me, and I in them, will produce much fruit. For apart from me you can do nothing" (John 15:5 NLT).

In my research, I learned a child takes responsibility for everything that goes wrong in their childhood, which results in a distorted, ingrained mindset, laced with demonic infiltration. Letting go and letting God is not something that comes easy to this programmed mindset as the subconscious mind will fight to stay in its comfort zone. Interestingly, many times the Christian community blames the demonic realm for tempting the flesh when it probably is the person's own habits, values, and beliefs, embedded in their soul/mindset, driving their behavior. The flesh is a strong contender against our desire to change even for good, more than we realize. That's why the Word tells us to be transformed by the renewing of our minds in Romans 12:2 and warns us about our behavior in Scripture and not giving the enemy a foothold. This is in line with what I heard once, "Sin will always take you further than you want to go, keep you longer than you want to stay, and cost you more than you want to pay!" The enemy of our souls knows this better than most Christians do.

There were many things I was delivered from after surrendering my life to the lordship of Jesus Christ, some right away and others over time, even up to the writing of this book. The earliest deliverance I recall is still so profound to me. The Lord removed profane language from my mouth on the day I was saved. It was as if He touched my tongue with His finger, and I never wanted to say another swear word again.

"He touched my lips with it and said, 'See, this coal has touched your lips. Now your guilt is removed, and your sins are forgiven'" (Isaiah 6:7 NLT).

Even today, if I use the appearance of a swear word, my family is surprised as it is not my practice. However, that was not always the case before the Lord touched me. I grew up hearing these words and subsequently using the F-word, B-word, N-word, and every other foul word as a noun, adjective, or verb in speaking to others, describing people, places, or situations. But after graduating from college in my first professional position and raising my daughters, I didn't want to use bad language anymore. I disciplined myself outwardly but could not inwardly. As the Bible reveals:

"These rules may seem wise because they require strong devotion, pious self-denial, and severe bodily discipline. But they provide no help in conquering a person's evil desires" (Colossians 2:23 NLT). I was helpless to change until I gave my life to the Lord on December 7, 2005, and He removed it from me. I didn't realize it then, but He replaced bad words from my tongue with His Word! I remember thinking, all I wanted to do was speak the Word in every conversation, plaster the Word on the walls of my home, and share the Word with everyone, everywhere I went. This was the Hand of God in my life! And what He did for me, He will do for you!

The Holy Spirit knows the strongholds and where the enemy has encamped in your soul. The Holy Spirit will be your guide to set you free. When the Holy Spirit shows you what to do such as memorizing scripture, repentance, prayer, and fasting, attending a prophetic or deliverance ministry, then do it. Also, you may need spiritual counseling, which is best administered through the work of the Holy Spirit, either directly or with another believer as the Scriptures reveal.

HOLY SPIRIT DIRECT COUNSELING:

When you pray and are alone with the Holy Spirit, there is no substitute! He will lead according to the Word of God and your prayer in line with God's will for you. He is the ultimate counselor who knows the truth about everything that has ever happened to you and your previous generations.

> "But the Helper (Comforter, Advocate, Intercessor-Counselor, Strengthener, Standby), the Holy Spirit, whom the Father will send in My name [in My place, to represent Me and act on My behalf], He will teach you all things, And He will help you remember everything I have told you" (John 14:26 AMP).

There was a time I prayed and asked the Lord how I was able to make good business decisions, but when it came to decisions of my heart, I fell apart! I remember writing on a yellow sticky note, "Lord, please help me to get unstuck." Within a few weeks, the Holy Spirit led and illuminated the following scripture during my reading:

"When I was a child, I talked like a child, I thought like a child, I reasoned like a child. When I became a man (in my case a woman), I put childish ways behind me" (1 Corinthians 13:11 NIV parenthetical added). When I finished reading, I had a supernatural encounter. The Lord sent me a vision and I could see myself as a child looking over my shoulder to see if someone was coming. Then the Holy Spirit spoke to me and gently said, "You have to let go of looking back. No one is coming!" This was a very painful and emotional encounter. It still brings tears to my eyes, even as I'm writing it, knowing how the Lord delivered me. This was the moment I was set free from the childlike fantasy of waiting, hoping beyond hope that someone was coming for me.

This was also the impetus through which the Holy Spirit led me to study and research human psychological development. I researched Erik Erickson, Sigmond Freud, and other behavioral psychological models. (Please note: I am not a licensed psychologist, psychiatrist, or doctor. I am a surrendered believer, a follower of Jesus Christ, so please pray and research this for yourself). When I read about all the things that could go wrong in a child's developmental upbringing, I was overwhelmed, even with what would be considered a normal childhood with loving parents. I knew not even the best psychologist could "pinpoint" or know exactly where a person is broken internally and needs healing. Just as we are intricately designed with the things we can see—our eyes, ears, nose, arms, legs, and internal organs—we are also intricately designed with the things we can't see—our spirit, soul, internal memory banks, will, and emotions. I remember concluding that only God who designed us knows exactly where we need healing and wholeness.

Another area in my mind where I was deeply held captive was the attachment bonding. I learned that bonding and attachment fall into two primary categories— secure and insecure. I presumed my attachment was insecure. But when I inquired of the Lord, the Holy Spirit revealed I had a trauma bond, much to my surprise. A trauma bond is formed when there is prolonged abuse, with a cycle of abuse and then remorse. Within the Dr. Jekyll/Mr. Hyde phenomenon, after causing harm, the abusive person may promise to change and be especially kind to make up for their behavior. This gives the abused person hope that their suffering will end and that they will one day receive the love or connection that the abuser has promised. This bond is not easily broken, as it is wired into the subconscious and unconscious mind, which keeps the person in an unrelenting repeated cycle that becomes more ingrained and carries into attracting future relationships that will continue the cycle. I was drawn into one toxic relationship after another until the marital relationship with the responsibilities of providing for a family, motherhood, love for my children, and keeping my family together brought me to the cross of Jesus Christ! Unbeknownst to me, this would be the beginning of the Holy Spirit breaking me free from the toxicity of the embedded trauma bond in my mind and behavior that held me captive.

The bond was so intricately woven within my soul that it required delicate spiritual surgery, which only the Holy Spirit could perform. My freedom would not have been possible without the Lord and the Holy Spirit preparing and leading me step by step to break free from the relational tendencies and demonic influence that fueled and secured the bond. I will share more details in Chapter Nine on Healing, Deliverance, and Restoration.

In addition to counseling alone with the Holy Spirit, the Word instructs us to counsel with one another. The Word works! I'm living proof, as well as many others that have been transformed by the Word of God!

COUNSELING WITH ANOTHER BELIEVER:

"Let the words of Christ, in all their richness, live in your hearts and make you wise. Use His words to teach and counsel each other. Sing psalms and hymns and spiritual songs to God with thankful hearts" (Colossians 3:16 NLT).

I needed someone to talk to about the things I had been through. I needed counseling but could not afford a Christian counselor at any price. So, in line with Scripture and led by the Holy Spirit, I asked a believing friend if she would come together in prayer to counsel me, and she agreed. I went to her home, and we prayed the Word and asked the Holy Spirit to reveal the truth. She set up her living room with the couch looking out of the window so that I wasn't facing her, and after we were done praying she said to speak the first thing the Holy Spirit brings to my mind. I said I was getting thoughts about my sister who died at ten months old from SIDS when I was about three years old. As I shared more information with her, she said what she believed the Holy Spirit was revealing to her about my situation. She told me I had never grieved the death of my sister and in my "child's" mind, she is still alive and I am trying to protect her. This made sense and aligned with my behavior of caring for my daughters. I recall family members saying I was overprotective, and my response was, "Well, I'd rather be overprotective than under-protective." But I knew in my heart, it was more than just being overprotective. There was something else that was driving my behavior. I couldn't bear the thought of leaving my daughters for a long period of time. When I was away from them, I felt very uneasy, anxious, and fearful. I remember when my youngest twin daughter had RSV (a newborn sickness). I stayed up all night watching to make sure she didn't stop breathing and that she stayed alive. After this counseling session, within the next couple of days, I was alone and had a time of intense weeping. I instinctively knew I was finally grieving the death of my sister and from that moment on the demonic oppression was lifted, my mindset was renewed, and my behavior began to change.

Do you need something lifted off of you? You may not know yourself, whether you do or not. If there is something you think is hidden and needs to be exposed, ask the Holy Spirit what the hidden things in your life are that drive your decisions and behavior.

You can pray a prayer similar to this:

Father, thank You for Your blessings and for revealing the truth through Your Word. Holy Spirit, please lead and guide me through the process of inner healing and counseling. Remove the blinders from my eyes so that I may see clearly the direction in which You are leading me. I ask this in the name of Jesus! Amen.

The Holy Spirit will lead you one step at a time toward complete exposure, healing, and deliverance and will connect you with other believers to help you through the process. Pray for discernment and clarity from the Holy Spirit before you move forward with another believer in counseling to be sure it is from the Lord. Any counseling session that does not evoke the Holy Spirit's presence and guidance is putting a band-aid on the problem and not getting to the root issue. A person can operate in their calling, profession, and giftings without having to acknowledge the Lord through repentance. This explains how a person can function in society on autopilot in their subconscious mind, even with a mangled dysfunctional soul that opposes the Lord, which is deeply hidden in their unconscious mind. This does not exclude pastors, believers, church members, business and governmental leaders, or anyone.

"The gifts and calling of God are without repentance" (Romans 11:29 NKJV).

"Not everyone who says to Me, 'Lord, Lord,' shall enter the kingdom of heaven, but he who does the will of my Father in heaven. Many will say to Me in that day, 'Lord, Lord, have we not prophesied in Your name, cast out demons in Your name, and done many wonders in Your name?' And then I will declare to them, 'I never knew you; depart from Me, you who practice lawlessness!'" (Matthew 7:21-23 NKJV).

We may be able to operate in our gifting in the world and church without repentance, but we will not be free from worldly lusts that lure us into sin, aided by the temptations of the enemy. These hidden behaviors will eventually rear their ugly head at some point and time in our life.

"The time is coming when everything that is covered up will

be revealed, and all that is secret will be made known to all" (Luke 12:2 NLT). Let's turn our attention to freedom from worldly lusts.

FREEDOM FROM WORLDLY LUSTS:

Like a lure on a hook to catch a fish or a trap in a cage to catch a wild animal, the world dangles many lures in front of us daily, and suffice it to say, we usually get caught in the trap before we even realize it. Not because the devil made us do it! But because we are drawn away by our own evil desires, and of course the devil couldn't be happier to entice us into our own sinful traps.

What is causing the quarrels and fights among you? Isn't it the whole army of evil desires within you? You want what you don't have, so you scheme and kill to get it. You are jealous for what others have, and you can't possess it, so you fight and quarrel to take it away from them. And yet the reason you don't have what you want is that you don't ask God for it. And even when you do ask, you don't get it because your whole motive is wrong—you want only what will give you pleasure. You adulterers! Don't you realize that friendship with the world makes you an enemy of God? I say it again, that if your aim is to enjoy this world, you can't be a friend of God. What do you think the scriptures mean when they say that the Holy Spirit, whom God has placed within us, jealously longs for us to be faithful? He gives us more and more strength to stand against such evil desires. As the scriptures say, "God sets himself against the proud, but he shows favor to the humble." (James 4:1-6 NLT)

What are worldly lusts? Every person has different worldly lusts that are synonymous with their natural family bloodline and personality that lure them into worldly traps. But there is one trap that seems to be universal for both Christians and non-Christians. Many people come from all over the world to the United States of

America in the hopes of attaining "the American Dream." Financial prosperity, large beautiful homes, expensive cars, prosperous businesses and careers, pleasurable living, and all the good things in life. What is behind the desire to obtain the American dream, to get caught in a trap? As even described in secular song lyrics. Scripture reveals it plainly:

> "For all that is in the world—the lust of the flesh, the lust of the eyes, and the pride of life—is not of the Father, but is of the world" (1 John 2:16 NKJV).

The pride of life and lust of the eyes and flesh can easily lead us down the wrong path. We can get caught up in sinful behaviors that entangle us and from which it becomes difficult to break free: greed, addictions, lies, deception, anger, bitterness, and others.

Leading up to surrendering my life to Jesus, there was a time when everything appeared to be going well, at least on the surface. I had a growing profitable business in the automotive manufacturing industry, was married with three beautiful daughters, a large home, rental property, and expensive cars, faithfully attended church on Sundays and was celebrated by the world around me. I had everything the world says should bring joy and happiness within my circle of influence; I was living "the American Dream"! I had what most people are still trying to get. As I was sitting in the great room of my home looking at the marble dining room set we hadn't used, thinking we needed a larger home, I thought, "What is wrong with me?" I was living in what would be considered the Taj Mahal, a palace, compared to the two-bedroom bungalow I grew up in. It wasn't adding up. It was the pride of life, the lust of the flesh and eyes that had me and my family in its grip, and without a supernatural intervention, breaking free would not have been possible!

The Holy Spirit, through early Bible studies, walked me

through letting go of the life I built on the sand, "the American Dream." I remember supernaturally seeing in my mind's eye a pile of sand in the shape of a large funnel. I was steadily trying to keep it up, yet no matter how fast my hands were moving, I couldn't keep it from falling. Finally realizing I could no longer hold it up on my own, I had to trust God every step of the way because it was coming down!

Anyone who listens to my teaching and obeys me is wise, like a person who builds a house on solid rock. Though the rain comes in torrents and the floodwaters rise and the winds beat against that house, it won't collapse, because it is built on rock. But anyone who hears my teaching and ignores it is foolish, like a person who builds a house on sand. When the rains and floods come and the winds beat against that house, it will fall with a mighty crash. (Matthew 7:24-27: NLT)

When I repented the day I was saved, that was the first step to begin building my house on the rock of Jesus Christ! Which, at the writing of this book, was 18 years ago when I was 39 years old. It would be a tough road ahead, as the Lord would bring down multiple idols in my life that were built on the sand. But that did not deter me because I no longer wanted to live the lie I had for so long and was looking forward to a better life that God had for me and my family.

HOW DO WE GET OUT AND STAY OUT OF WORLDLY LUSTS?

If you want freedom from worldly lusts, "repent" while you still can.

"For the kind of sorrow God wants us to experience leads us away from sin and results in salvation. There's no regret for that kind of sorrow. But, worldly sorrow, which lacks repentance, results in spiritual death" (2 Corinthians 7:10 NLT).

I believe, as Scripture reveals, there comes a point in a person's life when God will no longer grant repentance. Don't let that happen to you!

"...in humility, correcting those who are in opposition, if God perhaps will grant them repentance, so that they may know the truth" (2 Timothy 2:25 NKJV).

A situation that brought this to light for me was a family member that had once been a preacher of the Gospel, who had a drug addiction and was at the end of his life. While conversing with him, all he kept saying was that he just wanted to die. Under the inspiration of the Holy Spirit, I said, "You need to get face down on the ground and beg God to grant you repentance!" This is real and there is a consequence for those who continuously turn away from the Holy Spirit's conviction. "In those days, men will seek death and will not find it; they will desire to die, and death will flee from them" (Rev. 9:6 NKJV).

I called you so often, but you didn't come. I reached out to you, but you paid no attention. You ignored my advice and rejected the correction I offered. So, I will laugh when you are in trouble! I will mock you when disaster overtakes you—when calamity overcomes you like a storm, when you are engulfed by trouble, and when anguish and distress overwhelm you. I will not answer when they cry for help. Even though they anxiously search for me, they will not find me. For they hated knowledge and chose not to fear the LORD. They rejected my advice and paid no attention when I corrected them. (Proverbs 1: 24-30 NLT)

The Lord allowed me to come to a place in my life where I obtained what the world had to offer and encouraged success and prosperity, through hard work, tenacity, and perseverance, only to find it was baseless and empty without God as the foundation. It never delivered what it promised. In order for our life to have true meaning and fulfillment, it must be a surrendered life to God the Father, Jesus Christ, and the Holy Spirit! Otherwise, all that we can gain will come to naught in the end!

I recall several years after my salvation trying to keep what little was left of my business and providing for my daughters. There was a business deal that had the potential of generating enough income to keep me financially stable for a while as I cared for my children, but it was falling through. I remember coming under a serious spiritual attack. I began praying and talking with the Lord: "I know Your Word, and I shouldn't be this anxious. This is not of you. Help me, Holy Spirit, to see what is really going on. I prayed and read the Word, and the Holy Spirit illuminated this scripture:

> "No one can serve two masters. For you will hate one and love the other, or be devoted to one and despise the other. You cannot serve both God and money" (Matthew 6:24 NLT).

As soon as I read it, I said, "Lord, is this what's going on with me?" Without giving it another thought, I dropped down to my knees and repented to the Lord, and asked for forgiveness. At that moment, the anxiousness and demonic oppression in my mind were lifted. While I needed the money to pay my bills, what I needed more was to repent and be separated in my flesh from serving money over God. Within a couple of days, the deal came through, but now the money did not have the same hold on me, and I was praising and thanking the Lord, knowing it was His doing!

Get into the Word. Surrender to the lordship of Jesus Christ and the leading of the Holy Spirit. Obedience to the Holy Spirit will lead you to the exact scriptures and ministries you need for freedom within your soul to change your desires from worldly to godly. Repent and repent some more, for without repentance there is no remission of sin, and you will be subject to succumbing to worldly lusts.

> "And the world is passing away, and the lust of it; but he who does the will of God abides forever" (1 John 2:17 NKJV).

What happens when you've got the Word in you, you are not in any known sin, you've repented, are crucifying your flesh, and are obedient to the Holy Spirit, yet there seems to be another force pulling you in the opposite direction of the things of God? There's one place this is originating from and that is the demonic spiritual realm. We have to acknowledge spiritual infiltration in order to break free in the spirit realm. Much like a person who is addicted to drugs or alcohol, in order for that person to be free, they must first acknowledge the problem and then work toward eradicating it. Overcoming spiritual attacks is vital to the Christian life.

FREEDOM TO OVERCOME SPIRITUAL ATTACKS:

Spiritual attacks from demonic invisible forces are real. It's not a figment of your imagination. Once you surrender your life to the Lord, the enemy no longer has any control over you to possess you. There was an experience I had during the night a few months after I was saved. I thought it was a dream and woke up abruptly. I heard a voice within me speaking in an unknown language (tongues) and sensed there was a "spiritual" battle going on. I believe it was the Holy Spirit protecting me against demonic spiritual forces trying to come back to possess me. I really didn't want to know more, so I laid down and prayed and thanked God for protecting me.

While the enemy can no longer possess us when we are saved, he can and will do everything to infiltrate open doors and remain undetected in our souls' subconscious and unconscious realm and uncrucified flesh to oppress and demonize us.

"But Peter said, 'Ananias, why has Satan filled your heart to lie to the Holy Spirit and keep back part of the price of the land for yourself?'" (Acts 5:3 NKJV).

"But he turned and said to Peter, 'Get behind Me, Satan! You are an offense to Me, for you are not mindful of the things of God, but the things of men'" (Matthew 16:23 NKJV).

"I discipline my body like an athlete, training to do what it should. Otherwise, I fear that after preaching to others I myself might be disqualified" (1 Corinthians 9:27 NLT).

"And 'don't sin by letting anger control you.' Don't let the sun go down while you are still angry, for anger gives a foothold to the devil" (Ephesians 4:26-27 NLT).

The enemy's greatest weapon against humanity is deception and persistence in fortifying strongholds programmed into a person's mindset (rejection, fear, doubt, bitterness, lust, greed, and others) that are still present after salvation, without an immediate supernatural miraculous intervention. Humanity's greatest downfall is a lack of knowledge of the God of the Bible from early childhood.

"My people are destroyed for lack of knowledge" (Hosea 4:6a NKJV).

"Train up a child in the way he should go, and when he is old, he will not depart from it" (Proverbs 22:6 NKJV).

Spiritual warfare in and outside of the soul realm is usually triggered by one or more of the following:

1. Praying and standing in the gap for someone's salvation.
2. Praying for your own or someone's deliverance and pulling down strongholds.
3. Preaching, teaching, and prophesying the Gospel truth at your workplace, church, with your neighbor, at the grocery store, or anywhere else.

The enemy hates overcomers because they help others to overcome. If he can distort, distract, or delay your efforts, he will do his best to do so. When you use your freedom to help others break free, you become a prime target for the enemy with heightened attacks. If attacking you directly doesn't move you, the devil will attack the ones closest to your heart in an effort to keep you off of your mission. I've had first-hand experience.

However, everything can change when you surrender your life to the lordship of Jesus Christ and the Holy Spirit takes up residence inside of you. You will have the power within you that raised Jesus from the dead to overcome spiritual attacks, pull down strongholds, and expel demons from your life. But you will have to exercise your authority to do so.

"So humble yourselves before God. Resist the devil, and he will flee from you" (James 4:7 NLT)

Our right standing in Christ makes us an overcomer, but we must stand in the authority given to us by Christ. The price Jesus paid for our freedom and authority was His life, His shed blood.

Salvation doesn't cost us anything, but walking in our authority and living in true freedom will cost us dying to self, crucifying our flesh daily, and living a holy life. "Therefore, having these promises, beloved, let us cleanse ourselves from all filthiness of the flesh and spirit, perfecting holiness in the fear of God" (2 Corinthians 7:1 NKJV). Then the enemy is no match for the believer who walks in their authority and yields to the leading of the Holy Spirit.

> "And I have given you authority over all the power of the enemy, and you can walk among snakes and scorpions and crush them. Nothing will injure you. But don't rejoice just because evil spirits obey you; rejoice because your names are registered as citizens of heaven" (Luke 10:19-20 NLT).

True freedom is peace of mind and heart and is priceless, especially in uncertain times. It is peace in the face of tragedy, death, destruction, loss, and suffering, which can only be truly realized when you are in Christ.

> "I have told you all this so that you may have peace in me. Here on earth, you will have many trials and sorrows. But take heart, because I have overcome the world" (John 16:33 NLT).

Knowing who you are in Christ is a game changer, causing the enemies in your life to flee! Before we move on to the next chapter, pray for revelation of who you are in Christ!

Heavenly Father, thank You for sending Jesus to die on the cross for my sins. Open my spiritual eyes to see what I can't see, open my ears to hear what I can't hear, and receive the truth as You made available through reviving my spirit and the power of the Holy Spirit living inside of me. Help me to know who I am in Christ. I ask this in Jesus' name, Amen.

CHAPTER SEVEN

KNOWING WHO YOU ARE IN CHRIST

WHEN YOU SEE yourself in light of the Gospel and know in your heart through the infilling of the Holy Spirit what Jesus did for you by the shedding of His blood, making you righteous before God, you will be forever grateful and want to honor Him in all you do! You will have confidence on the inside that no one can take from you, whether you're at your job, at church, with unbelievers, or believers. In my first year of being saved and my first Bible study, I asked the leader a question on whether or not an action I took was a sin because I didn't want to sin against God. She said that it didn't matter because we were all "sinners" covered by grace. My immediate thought was, "Speak for yourself, I'm no longer a sinner," even though I still struggled with sin. I just knew I wasn't a sinner. Something changed in me. "Those who have been born into God's family do not make a practice of sinning, because God's life is in them. So they can't keep on sinning, because they are children of God" (1 John 3:9 NLT).

However, I didn't understand how it was possible to be righteous before God while still being an imperfect human being until later in my studies and revelation from the Holy Spirit.

"He made Christ who knew no sin to [judicially] be sin on our behalf, so that in Him we would become the righteousness of God [that is, we would be made acceptable to Him and placed in a right relationship with Him by His gracious lovingkindness]" (2 Corinthians 5:21 AMP).

Our righteousness doesn't come from anything that we can do but by faith in accepting the free gift of salvation of Jesus's death on the cross which makes us righteous before God!

"But it is from Him that you are in Christ Jesus, who became to us wisdom from God [revealing His plan and salvation], and righteousness [making us acceptable to God], and sanctification [making us holy and setting us apart for God], and redemption [providing our ransom from the penalty of sin], so then, as it is written [in Scripture], "He who Boasts and Glories, Let him boast and glory in the Lord" (1 Corinthians 1:30-31 AMP).

HOW DO YOU KNOW WHEN YOU KNOW WHO YOU ARE IN CHRIST?

As previously shared, there was a well-known preacher who had a very large following and many books on the New York Times Best Seller list, whose preaching was always encouraging and uplifting. Messages about how much God loves us and how He has a plan for our lives regardless of the sins we've committed, mistakes we've made, and so on. Hearing and accepting God's love for us, as we are, is foundational.

"For God so loved the world that He gave His only begotten Son, that whoever believes in Him should not perish but have everlasting life. For God did not send His Son into the world to condemn the world, but that the world through Him might be saved" (John 3:16-17 NKJV).

The Christian life is a spiritual journey, like going from preschool up through college and continuing education, with the exception that there is no set time for advancing between grade levels spiritually. The Lord prepares our pathway through the leading of the Holy Spirit to hear the written Word through local and media pastors, Bible studies, Christian books, ministries, music, and the like to guide us down our path toward wholeness and maturity. As we continually feed on the Word of God and submit to the leading of the Holy Spirit, we grow stronger and more confident in who we are in Christ. The purpose is to mature us to become more like Christ!

"For God knew his people in advance, and he chose them to become like his Son, so that his Son would be the firstborn among many brothers and sisters. And having chosen them, he called them to come to him. And having called them, he gave them right standing with himself. And having given them right standing, he gave them his glory" (Romans 8:29-30 NKJV).

There was a defining moment when I not only knew but stood up for who I was in Christ! It was in a conversation wherein I was being referred to in a derogatory manner, reminiscent of words I had been groomed to accept. But I was different now, no longer that little girl or the woman who was not equipped to defend herself, or just pass it off and accept such verbally abusive words against my personhood. I was now a woman of God who knew she was loved and cherished! I looked to my right and to my left and said to myself, "Who is this person talking to? Because it couldn't possibly be me. I'm bought and paid for by the blood of Jesus Christ!" So are you if you have made Jesus the Lord of your life!

The Lord used this circumstance not only to raise me to stand for who I was in Christ but to deflect the current potential wound and heal me from the wounds inflicted in my past by using my authority in Christ to stand up against the verbal attack.

When you begin to know who you are in Christ, you won't have to ask, "What does that mean to know who you are in Christ?" You will start loving yourself more than ever before from a godly perspective. You will not endure or allow ungodly behavior to be waged against you without a proper biblical response. You begin to measure yourself from the way that God sees you. You will know that you are loved so much because Jesus died for you so that you could be with Him for eternity! Knowing who you are in Christ gives you the courage to stand up for what you believe is true about who you are, free from the guilt and sin of your past, and to receive and live the blessings from above as written in the Word of God!

KNOWING WHO YOU ARE IN CHRIST LIBERATES YOU FROM THE NEED FOR PEOPLE'S APPROVAL

Putting the Word into action and relying on the Holy Spirit builds your confidence in your relationship with Christ. When you understand the value Jesus placed on your life deep within your heart and soul and His willingness to go to the cross on your behalf, people's approval or disapproval of you will pale in comparison. You will no longer need to justify your actions or behavior to anyone because you will know you have been justified by Christ alone!

"What then shall we say to these things? If God is for us, who can be against us? He who did not spare His own Son, but delivered Him up for us all, how shall He not with Him also freely give us all things? Who shall bring a charge against God's elect? It is God who justifies" (Romans 8:31-33 NKJV).

Not only that, but you'll stop expecting people to compensate you for what has happened or not happened to you. You will accept the price Jesus paid for you at the cross as full payment!

I was reading a chapter in a book about beauty for ashes, and I started talking to the Lord and said, "Where is my recompense for what I have gone through, what has happened to me?" And as clearly as I could hear in my spirit, the Lord said, "You got Me, Debra. I Am your recompense." I was immediately humbled! God is not only my recompense, but yours as well!

We are on our way to heaven, and whatever people or the enemy wage against us doesn't matter. When they talk about us behind our backs, ridicule or malign us, it will not change who we are, because we know who we belong to and who accepts us just as we are—God Almighty through the cross of Jesus Christ!

KNOWING WHO YOU ARE IN CHRIST EMPOWERS YOU TO WALK IN YOUR AUTHORITY

When you are in Christ, you will come up against opposition from people challenging who you are and your beliefs. At times it will be a natural opposition from friends, family, and others questioning what and why you believe what you do. Such as why you believe there's only one way to heaven through Jesus Christ. Then at other times, it will be supernatural opposition from the enemy, working through possessed non-believers and/or oppressed or demonized believers to challenge who you are in Christ using blatant accusations. While this can be divisive and unpleasant, knowing who you are in Christ will empower you to stand in your authority!

> "If the world hates you, you know that it hated Me before it hated you. If you were of the world, the world would love its own. Yet because you are not of the world, but I chose you out of the world, therefore the world hates you. Remember the word that I said to you, 'A servant is not greater than his master.' If they persecuted Me, they will also persecute you. If they kept My word, they will keep yours also" (John 15:18-20 NKJV).

Jesus made this very clear. If it happened to Him, it will happen to you. Knowing this should empower you to realize and understand it's not you personally they hate but the Jesus in you! This is cause to rejoice because they see Jesus in you! Hallelujah!

> "Blessed are you when people insult you, persecute you and falsely say all kinds of evil against you because of me. Rejoice and be glad, because great is your reward in heaven, for in the same way they persecuted the prophets who were before you" (Matthew 5:11 NIV).

When you are in Christ your response to such opposition should be to speak the truth in love! That is not always easy, but in Christ you are able! The Holy Spirit gave me clear direction early on, "If there is no Kingdom purpose, don't write or say anything." This was a mandate that my flesh did not like, nor the enemy of my soul. From that moment on, these words have been brought to my remembrance on many occasions, including the writing of this book. I've been careful to check my motives before saying or writing anything to ensure it was for Kingdom purposes. This can only be done through the act of crucifying the flesh and obedience to the Holy Spirit—through surrender! It is the Word and the Holy Spirit that gives us the power to crucify our flesh and turn away from the temptations of the enemy to stay in line with Kingdom purposes.

By his divine power, God has given us everything we need for living a godly life. We have received all of this by coming to know him, the one who called us to himself by means of His marvelous glory and excellence. And because of his glory and excellence, he has given us great and precious promises. These are the promises that enable you to share his divine nature and escape the world's corruption caused by human desires. (2 Peter 1:3-4 NLT)

We may not always get it right, but praise God His mercies are new every day! So, wake up in the morning and profess it is another day to walk with the Holy Spirit and get it right! When you know who you are in Christ and the Word gets down into your soul, you'll know when to say nothing and pray or reveal a truth that may sting or momentarily wound a friend.

> "Better is an open reprimand [of loving correction] than love that is hidden. Faithful are the wounds of a friend [who corrects out of love and concern], But the kisses of an enemy are deceitful [because they serve his hidden agenda]" (Proverbs 27:5-6 AMP).

It will be easier to be obedient to the direction of the Holy Spirit when you know who you are in Christ. Guidance from the Holy Spirit will be your first move. I remember a friend telling me that before saying or doing something, she would say to herself, "The Lord has done way too much for me to dishonor Jesus in what I want to say or do." When you know who you are in Christ and realize what Jesus did for you, you'll want to submit to His Will for you! You will use the sword for Kingdom purposes, not for your purposes, and you'll set the sword aside in obedience to the Holy Spirit's guidance.

KNOWING WHO YOU ARE IN CHRIST WILL GIVE YOU THE COURAGE TO BE YOUR TRUE SELF IN ALL OF YOUR RELATIONSHIPS

Apologizing for your bad behavior in relationships will come more easily when you know who you are in Christ. As you grow in your walk with the Lord, it will supernaturally become more natural to own your sinful behavior, apologize, and turn away from it.

> "Throw off your old evil nature and your former way of life which is rotten through and through, full of lust and deception. Instead, there must be a spiritual renewal of your thoughts and attitudes. You must display a new nature because you are a new person created in God's likeness–righteous, holy, and true" (Ephesians 4:22 NLT).

As I was growing in my relationship with Christ, there were many times my behavior needed complete change. Wrong behavioral patterns established early in my life (strongholds) would still emerge as it took time to transform and be delivered from implanted wrong values, beliefs, and perceptions kept away, hidden in the dark recesses of my unconscious mind. There were times I was aware that my behavior was out of line with biblical principles and at other times unaware. Those closest to me would let me know so that I would be more cognizant of the behavior and turn away from it. The Holy Spirit prompted me early on to ask for forgiveness whenever I did something wrong which contributed to my changing behavior from lack of patience to having patience, unrealistic demands to realistic expectations, hurtful words, and tones that were intimidating and fearful, to uplifting words and tones that were encouraging and faith-filled! They were instrumental in assisting me with biblical truth and their walk with the Lord to exhibit these behaviors. In addition, love buried deep in my heart drove me to my knees in prayer asking and at times begging God to help me to become better in my relationships both naturally and spiritually. Only with the Lord could this be possible!

Knowing who you are in Christ breaks off any pride or stubbornness that would keep you from asking for forgiveness from anyone, especially young children whom you may think as children, will get over it. Asking for forgiveness is the first step in helping them to get over it. I've even found myself asking for forgiveness from my small dog when I've not treated her right. Scripture has something to say about how we treat our animals. "The righteous care for the needs of their animals" (Proverbs 12:10a NIV). Whether it's your child, spouse, family, friend, or believer, acknowledging your wrongdoing frees you to be who you are in Christ!

When you know who you are in Christ you will also find yourself "supernaturally" changing who and where you spend your time. Establishing good boundaries with friends and family is very important as revealed in Scripture. "Don't be fooled by those who say such things, for 'bad company corrupts good character'" (1 Corinthians 15:33 NLT). You will not only have the courage to set boundaries but the strength and ability to keep them. You won't try to hide, cover up, or continue using a false self to make people like or love you, whether you're a student, business leader, pastor, minister, stay-at-home mother, wife, or husband. You will just be you. You will share who you truly are, the good, the bad, and the ugly, with those closest to you or with whomever the Holy Spirit leads you to share, knowing Jesus paid the price for you as you are! Your true self is the person that God knows and loves, not the false self.

Knowing who you are in Christ will allow your true self to emerge. You will have the courage to drop false selves constructed in your mind and imposters implanted by the enemy so that your true self can come out of hiding. Listen to the words of Jesus when He calls your true self unto Him: "Come to me, all you who labor and are heavy laden, and I will give you rest. Take My yoke upon you and learn from Me, for I am gentle and lowly in heart, and you will find rest for your souls. For My yoke is easy and My burden is light" (Matthew 11:28-30 NKJV).

It's a burden carrying a false self around, but in Christ, we can lay it down and start new in this life in preparation for eternity. You can be confident when you allow your true self to emerge and be transformed by the will of God that you are right in the middle of God's will for your life!

> "O Lord, You have searched me and known me. You know my sitting down and my rising up; You understand my thought afar off. You comprehend my path and my lying down, and are acquainted with all my ways. For there is not a word on my tongue, But, behold, O Lord, You know it altogether" (Psalm 139:1-4 NKJV).

When you know who you are in Christ, you will no longer pass the blame to the devil, a person, or a circumstance to cover your sin or continue in the false self. Rather, you'll be praising God for sending His only Son, Jesus, to die for your sins, and you'll willingly repent! You'll embrace who you really are, your true self who God created!

If you are aware of operating in a false self, pray and ask the Lord to help you come out of the false self you allowed and embrace your true self, who God loves and wants you to love as well!

Father, thank You for all You've done for me and for giving me the courage through my relationship with Jesus Christ to free my true self from deep down in my soul to come out and be excited about living the life You created for me to live. Thank You, Holy Spirit, for helping me to walk this journey. In Jesus' Name, Amen.

Knowing who you are in Christ will secure the way for your continued journey. Trials and suffering will come, but when you know who you are in Christ, you will make it through them and come out stronger and thriving on the other side, as we will discover in the next chapter.

CHAPTER EIGHT

UNCHARTED TERRITORY–
TRIBULATION VALLEY

WHEN YOU SURRENDER and walk with Jesus, it is inevitable that you will go through "tribulation valley." It may look different for each person, but it will be experienced. The truth is, whether or not you surrender your life to Jesus, you will more than likely experience tumultuous times, so it is better to go through them with Jesus and the Holy Spirit at your side! Going through tribulations ordained by the sovereignty of God will empower you to thrive on the other side! It's in the tough times that we really look up, realize our frailty, and examine ourselves. If we allow the Holy Spirit to do His work, then trials and tribulations will change us from the inside out! You can't hide, run, or escape from trials, tribulation, and suffering as they are a necessity for your life in Christ. "So even though Jesus was God's son, He learned obedience from the things He suffered" (Hebrews 5:8 NLT).

"Solid food is for those who are mature, who have trained themselves to recognize the difference between right and wrong and then do what is right" (Hebrews 5:14 NLT).

You may ask, "Why these fiery trials? What's really going on? When will it end?"

WHY THESE FIERY TRIALS?

"Dear friends, don't be surprised at the fiery trials you are going through, as if something strange were happening to you. Instead, be very glad—because these trials will make you partners with Christ in his suffering, and afterward you will have the wonderful joy of sharing his glory when it is displayed to all the world" (1 Peter 4:12-13 NLT).

WHAT'S REALLY GOING ON?

"And not only that, but we also glory in tribulations, knowing that tribulation produces perseverance, and perseverance, character, and character, hope. Now hope does not disappoint, because the love of God has been poured out in our hearts by the Holy Spirit who was given to us" (Romans 5:3-5 NKJV).

WHEN WILL IT END?

When God's purpose is fullfilled. It could be 24 hours, three days, 40 days, three and a half years, 15 years, and so on. To everything there is a season, a time for every purpose under heaven. (Ecclesiastes 3:1 NKJV).

God will prepare you not only to survive through trials, suffering, and tribulation but to thrive on the other side as you stay closely connected to the Holy Spirit who will guide you through hell and out if necessary! Prepare yourself, and know that the plans of God for your life are good, no matter what you are facing.

There are numerous tribulations we can find ourselves in the middle of. I believe the following are more common to every believer at some point and time in their spiritual journey. They are the tribulation of truth, the tribulation of relationships, the tribulation from the enemy, and God-ordained tribulation.

TRIBULATION OF TRUTH:

I remember as the truth began to be revealed in my life, I couldn't believe how long I had lived in the lies. As stated before, when you believe a lie, you live a lie! Honestly, when the time comes to step out of those lies, it can be very painful to walk away from them. Not only will you come under attack from the enemy to stay connected to the lie, but your own flesh (subconscious and unconscious mind) will fight you to keep you in your comfort zone of the lies you've believed ingrained in your soul. Going through the tribulation of truth is humbling. He stands against the proud and gives grace to the humble!

> "But He gives more grace. Therefore, he says: 'God resists the proud, But gives grace to the humble'" (James 4:6 NKJV).

> You're going to need His grace, so humble yourself as you go through the tribulation of truth!

"Remember it is better to suffer for doing good, if that is what God wants, than to suffer for doing wrong" (1 Peter 3:17 NLT).

The tribulation of truth will come to challenge the truth you have acquired against the real truth and wisdom only found in the Word of God. You'll see the truth but not everyone around you may be on board, and you could find yourself alone with the Holy Spirit in a tribulation of truth!

There was a movie in the 80s with a famous line, "YOU CAN'T HANDLE THE TRUTH!" That could not be stated any better for all of us, whether we admit it or not! When it comes to truth, most of us can't handle it. Especially when the truth is revealed to us about who we are in relation to a holy God and His holy Scriptures!

Stop fooling yourselves. If you think you are wise by this world's standards, you will have to become a fool so you can be wise by God's standards. For the wisdom of this world is foolishness to God. As the scriptures say, "God catches those who think they are wise in their own cleverness." And again, "The Lord knows the thoughts of the wise, that they are worthless." (1 Corinthians 3:18-19)

When this scripture was first illuminated in my reading, I thought, "That's me, Lord!" I thought I was clever and wise from a worldly perspective in my circle of influence with my little piece of the worldly pie. I thought I had all the answers, but when I read this scripture, my response was, "Make me a fool, Lord, so that I may become wise by your standards!" He did! It was painful to receive in my flesh but glorious to my spirit. I was learning and receiving truth like never before. The tribulation of truth comes when you clearly see things in the natural from a supernatural perspective about a person, place, or thing. You see childlike behavior in the adults around you, but they don't see it themselves. I believe Paul knew it when he penned to an audience of adults: "Little Children, it is the last hour; and as you have heard that the Antichrist is coming, even now many antichrists have come, but which we know that it is the last hour" (1 John 2:18 NKJV). "And now, little children, abide in Him, that when He appears, we may have confidence and not be ashamed before Him at His coming" (1 John 2:28 NKJV).

You begin to recognize the false idols you put up in your life as you see others still in this same trap. The religious activities in which you once participated that are unbiblical can be tough truths to realize. Even recognizing lies at a funeral home. You never go to a funeral and hear, "Oh, well that person surely went to hell." No, in the funeral home, it appears everyone is going to heaven; at least that has been my experience. But that's just not so. As I walked closely with the Holy Spirit, I was given revelation to be able to see the difference between a person who belonged to the Lord versus the world, even at the funeral.

> "The person with the Spirit makes judgments about all things, but such a person is not subject to merely human judgments, for 'Who has known the mind of the Lord so as to instruct him?' But we have the mind of Christ" (1 Corinthians 2:15-16 NIV).

The tribulation of truth begins when you realize you've been living a lie and don't understand how you could have lived it for so long, and now you're surrounded by lies.

The lies you've believed get entangled in your mind like intertwined connections. You will need spiritual surgery that only comes from Doctor Jesus through the work of the Holy Spirit, to unravel, dislodge, remove, and rewire new godly truth connections (electrons) in your mind. It may happen supernaturally through deliverance from demonic oppression, possession, and/or demonization, but transforming your mind usually happens over time. Sometimes the only way is through tribulation valley, but take heart! Jesus is the author and the finisher of our faith!

> "Looking unto Jesus, the author and finisher of our faith, who for the joy that was set before Him endured the cross, despising the shame, and has sat down at the right hand of the throne of God" (Hebrews 12:2 NKJV).

Midway through my journey, we were moving from one house to another. I was working less than part-time in my business, which was at an all-time low. My primary responsibility was taking care of my daughters and being obedient to the Holy Spirit's direction. We were down to one leased vehicle, as our two other vehicles had been repossessed.

A family member came over to visit and was really beside themselves as they saw I was riding a bicycle with a carriage to carry my twin daughters while my oldest rode her bike as we would go to a nearby park for daily picnic lunches. They were distraught by my lifestyle as it was digressing. I went from being able to shop at Sax Fifth Avenue to not being able to afford the Salvation Army. They called me after leaving our home and said, "You better go to work because you're going to have to move again." They said, "Christian's work. Do you know that?" I said, "I do, but God told me to focus on taking care of my children, and I'm going to do what God told me." They said, "How long is it going to last?" I said, "I don't know. However long God decides." They said, "You don't know how long it will last?" I said, "No, I don't." They said, "All you want to do is read that Bible, and you and your family are going to end up in a shelter." I said, "If that's where God wants us to go, then that's where we will go! I am going to do what God tells me to do, no matter what!" I said, "Listen, if this is too difficult for you to handle, then don't call me; I'll call you when it's over." They said, "When is that going to be?" I replied, "I don't know. You have to understand, I am doing what God tells me to do!"

I remember a subsequent phone call where they were urging me to do something to change my situation and warning me of what was to come. I truly didn't want to hurt anyone and really didn't want to continue experiencing what we were going through, but I knew in my heart I was trusting God and following the leading of the Holy Spirit. When the phone call ended, the Holy Spirit brought to my memory the following scripture:

> "If you love your father or mother more than you love me, you are not worthy of being mine; or if you love your son or daughter more than me, you are not worthy of being mine. If you refuse to take up your cross and follow me, you are not worthy of being mine" (Matthew 10:37-38 NLT).

While driving in my car, I responded, "Lord, this is not easy for me. I don't want my family to end up in a shelter, but I'll go wherever you lead." This was a pivotal moment and a difficult truth to face and accept, but it was necessary to go on with Christ, not only for my life but for my family's life. I knew the only way I would make it was to follow Jesus! I believe the Lord kept me from Christian leaders that would try to talk me out of what God was walking me through, and today I'm thankful for it!

The tribulation of truth comes when you start experiencing firsthand the "real" truth of human nature. Because of my experiences, I was starting to deeply understand what Jesus was referring to in the following passages: "Another of his disciples said, 'Lord, first let me return home and bury my father.' But Jesus told him, 'Follow me now! Let those who are spiritually dead care for their own dead'" (Matthew 8:21-22 NLT).

"Don't imagine that I came to bring peace to the earth! No, I came to bring a sword. I have come to set a man against his father, a daughter against her mother, and a daughter-in-law against her mother-in-law. Your enemies will be right in your own household!" (Matthew 10:34-36-37 NLT).

I was experiencing pushback and warfare firsthand in every direction as I was coming out of religious idolatry. Let me tell you, the Devil was rearing his ugly head, and the warfare at times was relentless. Tribulation of truth comes the day you become aware that you placed your trust in the wrong person, place, or thing, and now you know it, but they don't.

"But Jesus didn't trust them, because he knew what people were really like. No one needed to tell him about human nature" (John 2:24-25 NLT).

I remember walking through many tribulations of truth and receiving revelations from the Holy Spirit about my circumstances. At one point, I said to myself, "I just had to know, didn't I? It wasn't enough for me to mind my own business. Maybe if I had, I wouldn't be going through this right now." But I didn't allow these thoughts to simmer within me. There was no turning back. I was going on with God! For as Jesus said, "No one, having put his hand to the plow, and looking back, is fit for the Kingdom of God" (Luke 9:62 NKJV).

The more I studied, learned, and applied the Word, the more truth I received! Thank God! I never wanted to go back to the lie that we lived and didn't want my daughters to live the lie in their lives. I prayed for strength to keep going forward, and through the power of the Holy Spirit, it was given! "I can do all things through Christ who strengthens me" (Philippians 4:13 NKJV)! Don't put your head in the sand because the Tribulation of truth hurts! The tribulation of truth also heals! God will not fail you! Love doesn't fail and God is Love! "He who does not love does not know God, for God is Love" (1 John 4:8 NKJV).

TRIBULATION OF RELATIONSHIPS:

When the light of the Holy Spirit gets brighter within you, the darkness around you is revealed.

"Can two walk together unless they are agreed?" (Amos 3:3 NKJV).

This is a rhetorical question. You don't have to be a Bible scholar to know that the answer is, "No!" Something happens in the supernatural when you begin to follow Jesus and those around you, your friends and family are not. "Of course, your former friends are surprised when you no longer plunge into the flood of wild and destructive things they do" (1 Peter 4:4a NLT)

It is a natural, supernatural separation that you will experience. It can be lonely if you are the first coming out of the old and into the new. I began to make Bible friends and could relate rather closely to King David in many of the Psalms he wrote about the relationship issues he experienced.

When you find yourself ensnared in a relationship under the control of the enemy, whether it's a friend, boyfriend, husband, family member, or someone else, sometimes there's only one way out and that is through, with of course, the guidance of the Holy Spirit and Word of God. Relationship abuse comes in many shapes and sizes. Verbal and emotional abuse is as harmful to the mind, heart, and soul as outward forms of abuse. However, before ever contemplating a relationship separation or divorce, you should take every step directed in Scripture to restore or revive the relationship through Christian counseling, prayer, fasting, and following the leading of the Holy Spirit.

(However, if you're in an abusive relationship that is life-threatening, you need to separate immediately and seek police protection and godly support). God knows the beginning from the end and will prepare a way when there seems to be no way.

> "Do not remember the former things, Nor consider the things of old. Behold I will do a new thing, Now it shall spring forth; Shall you not know it? I will even make a way in the wilderness and rivers in the desert" (Isaiah 43:18-19 NKJV).

The Word tells us to do good to those who spitefully use us and to love those who persecute us. It also tells us to be careful with whom we associate. In fact, the Bible has a lot to say about the type of people we should avoid. You can love them from a distance and sometimes that's the best way. "I urge you, brothers and sisters, to watch out for those who cause divisions and put obstacles in your way that are contrary to the teaching you have learned. Keep away from them; for such people are not serving our Lord Christ, but their own appetites. By smooth talk and flattery, they deceive the minds of naïve people..." (Romans 16:17-19 NIV).

The tribulation of a relationship will come when you begin putting up healthy boundaries, much to the dismay of the other person. There may be times when you clearly know by the leading of the Holy Spirit and the Word that you have to end a toxic relationship with someone you're attached to.

Since being saved in 2005, I've walked through several heart-piercing relationship separations. As my walk began to grow in Christ and my light got brighter, it exposed the darkness in relationships around me. Not everyone who claims to be a Christian is, as the Bible states. But you are not controlled by your sinful nature. You are controlled by the Spirit if you have the Spirit of God living in you. And remember that those who do not have the Spirit of Christ living in them are not Christians at all. (Romans 8:9 NLT). As I was separating from these kinds of relationships, it felt like I was walking a tightrope. I had to hear from the Lord daily to know what next step to take. The tribulation and consequences of making a wrong move were heightened as other people's lives were affected by my decisions. If not for the Holy Spirit, I would not have survived walking through it. The only true hope is in Christ, who can bring beauty from ashes if we allow Him!

As I was learning to follow Jesus and His Word, I was teaching my daughters to do the same and each gave their life to Christ at a young age. The Word was strengthening me internally, and I was growing in the truth and knew I needed deliverance. God's Word and the Holy Spirit were the answer. Ultimately, there was a price to pay and a difficult walk of endurance. As I was getting delivered and set free from wrong thinking patterns, behavior, demonic oppression, and toxic relationships, many times being carried through each step by the Lord, it was beyond challenging, and I would not have made it on my own.

I prayed and asked the Lord for protection and the Holy Spirit had me write this scripture: "I lift up my eyes to the mountains—where does my help come from? My help comes from the Lord, the Maker of heaven and earth. He will not let your foot slip—he who watches over you will not slumber" (Psalm 121:1-3 NIV).

As I pushed forward, there were rough waters to navigate. I remember driving when tears were pouring out of my eyes so much that the traffic light was blurred. I had to keep trusting God at His Word, the Holy Spirit, and believe. This was the road to life, even though it was very difficult!

"Enter by the narrow gate: for wide is the gate and broad is the way that leads to destruction, and there are many who go in by it. Because narrow is the gate and difficult is the way which leads to life, and there are few who find it" (Matthew 7:13-14 NKJV).

TRIBULATION FROM THE ENEMY:

Once you decide to start seeking God and surrender your life to the lordship of Jesus Christ, the Devil and his cohorts wake up to your new position and will begin their assault against you. They will wage attacks from isolated minor ones to serious ones that fall into the tribulation category. But know this: they are on God's leash and can only do what God allows them to do. If they had it their way, they would take us all out at once. It's important to understand the difference between an attack and tribulation. An attack is defined as an attempt to inflict harm. To set upon with violent force. To criticize strongly or in a hostile manner.

Tribulation is defined as distress or suffering resulting from oppression or persecution; a trying experience. Great affliction, trial, or distress, suffering. An experience that tests one's endurance, patience, or faith.

In the book of Revelation, beginning in chapter eight, it states the seventh seal is the prelude to the "seven trumpets" which begins the tribulation period. The first six trumpets bring tribulation to the earth. The first trumpet—vegetation is struck, the second trumpet—sea is struck, the third trumpet—waters are struck, the fourth trumpet—heavens are struck, the fifth trumpet—The locusts from the bottomless pit are released. "Then out of the smoke locusts came upon the earth. And to them was given power, as the scorpions of the earth have power. They were commanded not to harm the grass of the earth, or any green thing, or any tree, but only those men who do not have the seal of God on their foreheads. And they were not given authority to kill them, but to torment them for five months" (Rev. 9:3-5a NKJV).

The sixth seal—the angels from the Euphrates killed one-third of mankind. "But the rest of mankind who were not killed by these plagues, did not repent of the works of their hands, that they should not worship demons, and idols of gold, silver, brass, stone, and wood, which can neither see nor hear nor walk. And they did not repent of their murders and sorceries or their sexual immorality or their thefts" (Rev. 9:20-21 NKJV). Hence the seventh and final trumpet is the prelude to the bowl judgments or God's wrath on mankind.

We may not be around to go through this tribulation as detailed in the book of Revelation, but we can experience a tribulation in our own life when we surrender it all and follow Jesus. Jesus said, "If you cling to your life, you will lose it; but if you give up your life for me, you will find it" (Matthew 10:39 NLT). It can be quite a tribulation when you start to lose the life you once knew. When your family and friends no longer want to be around you and even turn against you, when you lose your possessions and the places where you once placed your worth. When your career, job, vocation, degrees, and diplomas are dismantled before your eyes. Your former places of worship will be revealed to you as well, where you thought you had a firm standing in God's kingdom, only to find it was the enemy's stronghold. This and other scenarios can become our tribulation. Many disciples of Jesus find themselves in these very places and situations. Of course, the enemy of our souls doesn't waste the opportunity. The attacks will escalate as your walk with the Lord grows, but God in His sovereignty has a plan and purpose for all of it. Sometimes, you'll need to just be still and know that He is God! (Psalm 46:10 NIV). Even so, that won't deter the enemy of your soul. He doesn't go on vacation, take a day off or a personal day. And a sick day is his best day if he can inflict it on a follower of Jesus Christ. The tribulation from the enemy comes to do exactly what we're told in Scripture: "The thief does not come except to steal, and to kill, and to destroy" (John 10:10a NKJV).

When the tribulation of the enemy comes, remember the words of Jesus: "I have come that they may have life, and that they may have it more abundantly" (John 10:10b NKJV). The enemy intends to destroy your relationships, first with God, spouse, brothers and sisters in Christ, family, and friends. Hell hates the "Overcomer" and will throw whatever they can against you to keep you from advancing the Kingdom of Light. The Word tells us, "And they overcame him by the Blood of the Lamb and the word of their testimony, and they did not love their lives to the death" (Rev. 12:11 NKJV). We are more than conquerors through Jesus Christ our Lord. No matter what battle you find yourself in, remember the battle belongs to the Lord, and He will fight for you. You are now His child, and He will do what His Word says—watch you with His eye. "I will instruct you and teach you in the way you should go; I will guide you with My eye" (Psalm 32:8 NKJV).

GOD ORDAINED TRIBULATION

Every test and tribulation the Lord sends is designed to bring renewal and change from our former way of life to the newness of life in Christ. Tribulation produces characteristics in us that we otherwise would not have or know. It produces dependence and trust in God and God alone. We learn obedience and the fear of the Lord. It prepares us for our heavenly home.

The book of Revelation speaks about tribulation to come, but we can experience a tribulation of our own that is God-ordained with loss, heartache, sorrow, suffering, and pain. In my first seven years of being saved, I experienced loss on a scale that I would not have imagined. My beautiful family home went into foreclosure, rental property was foreclosed, vehicles were repossessed, and business assets were seized and later stolen. I filed for bankruptcy and total liquidation. My million dollar business declined to complete dissolution. I was on the welfare line for food stamps and many of my family relationships and friendships have dissolved. I went from affording clothing at high-end department stores to receiving used clothing for myself and my daughters. Through these events, I was distressed, depressed, bewildered, astonished, stunned, and very introspective. My only hope for survival was having the Bible at my side every step of the way and being sensitive to following the leadership of the Holy Spirit. Otherwise, I would not have survived nor would I be here today writing about it. My two anchor scriptures were and still are:

> "Trust in the Lord with all your heart; do not depend on your own understanding. Seek His will in all you do, and He will show you which path to take" (Proverbs 3:5-6 NLT). "And we know that God causes everything to work together for the good of those who love God and are called according to His purpose for them" (Romans 8:28 NLT).

Here's a biblical description of the surrendered life, which I can attest to in my own life...

> "We are hard-pressed on every side, yet not crushed; we are perplexed, but not in despair; persecuted, but not forsaken; struck down, but not destroyed—always carrying about in the body the dying of the Lord Jesus, that the life of Jesus also may be manifested in our body"

(2 Corinthians 4:8-10 NKJV). "Therefore, we do not lose heart. Even though our outward man is perishing, yet the inward man is being renewed day by day. For our light affliction, which is but for a moment, is working for us a far more exceeding and eternal weight of glory, while we do not look at the things which are seen, but at the things which are not seen. For the things which are seen are temporary, but the things which are not seen are eternal" (2 Corinthians 4:16-18 NKJV).

Suffering and trials through tribulations produce character pleasing to God when we are surrendered to the lordship of Jesus Christ. While we would rather not have to go through trials, tribulation, and suffering, it is a part of life for the believer. I would rather walk through the trials, tribulations, and suffering in this life with Jesus than without Him. I have experienced both, and having Jesus makes all the difference in healing, deliverance, and restoration on the other side, as we'll learn in the next chapter.

CHAPTER NINE

HEALING (∿DELIVERANCE) & RESTORATION

THE ULTIMATE PHYSICIAN is Jesus and the power of the Holy Spirit works in you and through you. Healing and deliverance usually go hand in hand, and restoration follows. They are byproducts of the transformation in your life that begins the moment you surrender to the lordship of Jesus Christ and submit to the Holy Spirit!

The anchors for your spiritual journey are repentance and love! Each step taken on your journey fosters your healing, deliverance, and restoration.

You might ask, "What are we being healed (delivered) from?"

We are being healed from the soulish wounds acquired along the path of life, from being born with a sinful nature and living in a fallen world with an ongoing spiritual battle for our souls. Distortions and lies in our soulish realm may be hidden from our consciousness, deeply ingrained in our unconscious mind, including dysfunctions acquired through early childhood soul development from rejection and all of its abusive forms—physical, verbal, emotional, sexual, neglect, and abandonment. There may be wounds in our hearts and emotions from being unloved and distortions planted in our minds by those in authority influenced by the enemy. There may also be physical ailments from supernatural oppression and emotional distortions, resulting in natural manifestations.

> "When evening had come, they brought to Him many who were demon-possessed. And He cast out the spirits with a word, and healed all who were sick, that it might be fulfilled which was spoken by Isaiah the prophet, saying: 'He Himself took our infirmities and bore our sicknesses'" (Matthew 8: 16-17 NKJV).

Then you may ask, "What are we being restored to?"

We are being restored to a right relationship with God the Father, escaping His wrath through faith in the shed blood of Jesus Christ and the work of the Holy Spirit!

> "For God presented Jesus as the sacrifice for sin. People are made right with God when they believe that Jesus sacrificed His life, shedding His blood. This sacrifice shows that God was being fair when He held back and did not punish those who sinned in times past, for he was looking ahead and including them in what He would do in this present time. God did this to demonstrate His righteousness, for He Himself is fair and just, and He makes sinners right in his sight when they believe in Jesus" (Romans 3:25-26 NLT).

And Jesus came and spoke to them, saying, "All authority has been given to Me in heaven and on earth. Go therefore and make disciples of all the nations, baptizing them in the name of the Father and of the Son and of the Holy Spirit" (Matthew 28:18-19 NKJV).

The Word of God is medicine for everything your soul needs! For those who believe it, they will receive it. When you study, memorize, meditate, and apply Scripture to your life as the Holy Spirit leads, the Word will expose deep places within you where hurt and lies reside, and heal you!

> "For the Word of God is quick, and powerful, and sharper than any two-edged sword, piercing even to the dividing asunder of soul and spirit, and of the joints and marrow, and is a discerner of the thoughts and intents of the heart" (Hebrews 4:12 KJV).

HEALING (DELIVERANCE) IN YOUR HEART

Do you want to know what is really going on inside of you? Then listen to what you are saying. The Bible says that what comes out of your mouth is actually from the overflow of your heart.

> "What goes into someone's mouth does not defile them, but what comes out of their mouth, that is what defiles them" (Matthew 15:11 NIV).

God knows where you need to be healed and delivered in your heart, so what was previously there will no longer defile you.

> "But the things that come out of a person's mouth come from the heart, and these defile them. For out of the heart come evil thoughts—murder, adultery, sexual immorality, theft, false testimony, slander" (Matthew 15:18-19 NIV).

"A good man brings good things out of the good stored up in his heart, and an evil man brings evil things out of the evil stored up in his heart. For the mouth speaks what the heart is full of" (Luke 6:45 NIV).

I remember the first time this scripture really hit me, and I started monitoring what was coming out of my mouth. It shook me to the core as there were things I was saying in my private time that I would never want to get out or be repeated. Then I realized, "Oh my goodness, this is what's in my heart." I cried out to God, "Get it out, Lord! Create in me a clean heart!"

"Create in me a clean heart, O God, and renew a steadfast spirit within me" (Psalm 51:10 NKJV).

A clean heart only comes from the hands of God the Father, through Jesus Christ and submission to the Holy Spirit. People may try to fool you, but when you are submitted to the Holy Spirit, they will not be able to. The Holy Spirit will reveal it to you, and having discernment will help you to distinguish between good and evil. I heard a minister say once, "It is not the evil of the evil that will deceive the elect; it is the good of the evil!" There are people who look really good on the outside. They know how to say and do all the right things, including pastors, teachers, evangelists, ministers, family, and friends. But on close examination by the Spirit on the inside, they are far from good!

"Watch out for false prophets. They come to you in sheep's clothing, but inwardly they are ferocious wolves. By their fruit you will recognize them. Do people pick grapes from thornbushes, or figs from thistles?" (Matthew 7:15-16 NIV).

HEALING (DELIVERANCE) IN YOUR MIND AND EMOTIONS

It's not just the enemy of our souls that distorts our thinking but our own sinful nature (our flesh) with which we were born. Not only our thinking but our emotions as well! The thoughts, values, the ideas we learned, believed and stored within us from our family of origin, parents, friends and classmates, and others along the way. Our personal and worldly experiences play a significant role in our soul development that will have lasting effects on the outcome of our lives for better or worse. We can fly off the handle, cry without warning, anger flares up in an instant, and at a moment's notice we can turn it around. Everyone wants to say, "The devil made me do it!" Or, "I wouldn't have done that if it wasn't for that person or what happened to me." But the truth is, we're inclined to do wrong whether or not we believe someone else is pulling our strings. Let it be known, no one can bring anything out of you that's not already in you, including before any wrongdoing was ever perpetrated against you. "Where do wars and fights come from among you? Do they not come from your desires for pleasure, that war in your members? You lust and do not have. You murder and covet and cannot obtain. You fight and war. Yet you do not have because you do not ask. You ask and do not receive, because you ask amiss, that you may spend it on your pleasure" (James 4:1-2 NKJV).

But God has a plan and spiritual pathway designed specifically with you in mind, to bring healing right where you need it and to separate you from the sin inside you, the enemy that taunts you, and the world that lures you.

In early summer of 2019, the Lord impressed upon my heart to visit a family member out of state. I remember the Lord speaking in my spirit saying, "I'm sending you there to heal you." Given the nature of the relationship, I wasn't sure what I needed healing from as I believed I had forgiven from my heart. However, I was going with that in mind. During this encounter there was a move in the Spirit and I heard the Holy Spirit reveal to me that this person couldn't do anything for me, but I could do something for them. This brought forth repentance and my releasing forgiveness and love from deep within my soul.

Shortly after, I had a grand mal seizure, the first seizure I've ever had! I woke up in an ambulance and my husband was there and said, "We're taking you to the hospital to get you checked out." I wondered what happened. I had no memory of it. After the CT scans, they could not find anything wrong. A few hours later, I was back, seemingly fine. After we returned home, follow-up doctor's visits and all tests came back normal. The neurologist said it was brought on by stress. I thought, "Really? My whole life has been a stress case as a small business owner in the automotive manufacturing industry and many personal issues since birth. There's no way it was just stress." I began to pray and ask the Lord to reveal to me what happened. I remember He told me he was sending me there to heal me. The Lord revealed it as I was reading a book about loving as if you've never been hurt before by a well-known pastor in Georgia. The chapter I was reading gave an account of what happened just before Jesus died on the cross, when he said, "Father, forgive them, for they do not know what they do" (Luke 23:34 NKJV). The book went on to state that in one hour, forgiveness saved the world. God's hands will not touch spirits that do not release forgiveness. Wherever you release forgiveness, you release the power of the Spirit of God. It stated that when Jesus released forgiveness and finally died on the cross, heaven and earth collided. The earth shook. The veil of the temple was torn in two. The rocks were split in half. Graves were torn open. When you forgive, you also release the power of victory over the devil. But more importantly, when we forgive, we release God's power in our lives to bring healing. I knew this is what happened to me. As I released forgiveness, the unforgiveness I carried in my mind from childhood was released and the neurons in my brain went off like fireworks, and the demonic infiltration was lifted in this area of my mind. Also, I would later learn that the Lord provided for my miraculous healing through the laying on of hands and praying in the Spirit.

God wants to heal us. It doesn't matter where you are; when you're obedient to the Holy Spirit's prompting, He will make a way for your healing.

Is there somebody you have to forgive today? Don't waste another moment; go, and ask for forgiveness if you are able, or you can forgive from a distance if the relationship is toxic. If the person doesn't want to restore a relationship, or if they are deceased, you can still forgive or ask for forgiveness by writing it down and either mailing or not mailing a letter or email. Forgiveness is from the heart, and that is what matters to God. He wants to heal us from the things that defile us, to restore us back to our rightful relationship with Him. That is why Jesus came and died for our sins. So that we could be made right with God through faith alone in what He did for us. All we have to do is receive your healing (deliverance) and restoration.

RESTORATION:

Love is the restoration factor. We are restored to love!

> "And you shall love the Lord your God with all your heart, with all your soul, with all your mind, and with all your strength.' This is the first commandment. And the second, like it, is this: 'You shall love your neighbor as

yourself.' There is no other commandment greater than these" (Mark 12:30-31 NKJV).

Restoration comes in several ways. Here are a few ways we are restored to relationships, wholeness, and purpose.

RESTORED RELATIONSHIP(S):

Love is the bond that restores relationships, first our relationship with God and then with people. The most important relationship to be restored is with God the Father, and the only way is through faith in the shed blood of Jesus Christ and infilling of the Holy Spirit. When this relationship is restored, all other relationships will fall into place. The relationship with God is restored at the cross when we bend our knees, acknowledge our sins, and ask for forgiveness. It grows stronger as we grow in our faith in God, Jesus, and follow the leading of the Holy Spirit.

Know this—all sin that is committed can be traced back to an offense toward God. For example, when we are arrogant, prideful, and/or rebellious, thinking we're better than other people by how we look, dress, our intellect, giftings, spiritual wisdom, and social or financial status, we put ourselves on the same level as God! But once we're surrendered, He won't leave us that way, and conviction will soon come. I remember a time at a women's event when these two ladies who had less-than-desirable outward personalities and appearances came to the event. My first thought when I saw them at the door was, "Please, Lord, don't let them sit next to me." Of course, they squeezed in and pulled up another chair so that they both could sit, one on each side. The Lord spoke to me in my spirit and said, "Debra, don't reject what I've accepted!" That was profound for me, and I repented. It stayed with me as a reminder through the years! Restoration comes as we grow in our love walk.

"Be completely humble and gentle; be patient, bearing with one another in love" (Ephesians 4:2 NIV).

"Most important of all, continue to show deep love for each other, for love covers a multitude of sins" (1 Peter 4:8 NLT).

It was three and a half years before I had even gone out to coffee with another man since my divorce proceedings. I wasn't looking for a mate or even believed that true love was possible on this side of heaven. Then the Lord surprised me. He crossed my path with the man of my heart's desire on a Southwest flight from Chicago to Detroit on October 10, 2012. We were both traveling for business, and I ended up sitting in the middle seat next to him, being one of the last few people to board the flight. After a small conversation about our business ventures, we began sharing our faith. Then I asked the Lord, "Did you set this up?" Being uncertain, we exchanged business cards and the rest is history. We were married about a year and a half later, traveling back and forth from Nashville to Detroit every weekend until I moved with my daughters to Nashville in August of 2021. I had presumed the Lord was raising me back up in business, but little did I know He had other plans! He was restoring me to love in my heart, and not so coincidentally for my husband as well. God knew exactly what we needed—to be loved for who we were, not for what we could offer in terms of finances, nothing more and nothing less than our true selves, with no ulterior motives but to delight in loving and caring for each other. We were like teenagers in love in mid-life with his four and my three children, and we knew this was God who made it happen. We would say to each other, "I love Jesus more because of you in my life." The time I took to be alone with Jesus prepared me for this relationship as well as for him. I wasn't looking for a man to do something for me, but a mate to walk through life together, honoring God, and that's what we've been doing. The Lord brought us together to draw us closer to Him and heal our unloved hearts!

RESTORED TO WHOLENESS:

God restores us to His original plan as written in His Word for our life because of His great love for us! He leads us back to embracing who we are and who He created us to be. To receive and give love! He mends the fragmented parts of our personalities that were distorted. He heals our broken hearts from suffering and loss. Through sanctification, He separates us from the sinful nature we were born with.

For most of my life, I was trying to fill and satisfy a deep wound and unmet need for love in my heart. My attempts to fill the gaping hole only resulted in more heartbreak and disappointment. I was in an endless pursuit of success, driven by relentless attempts to prove my worth. My outward displays of excellence and success were byproducts of ultimately trying to win peoples love and approval and cover my inward deficiencies. For years, my childhood trauma kept a tight lid on my own sinful behavior under the protective coating. The behaviors we were born with as the Bible tells us, "We were born with an evil nature" (Ephesians 2:3b NLT). I justified my sinful actions accordingly. When the preacher said to forgive as you've been forgiven, I thought, "That's easy for you to say. You walk in my shoes, and then tell me how you forgave." What I went through wasn't fair or just, so I reasoned that I'll do what I want, when I want, and with whom I want, and it's no one's business. Except, there would be consequences, which had lifelong effects, and it is God's business because He is the one who made me and has been there from the beginning. When I was far from God, I would say over and over again to myself, "Why did You do this to me? Why did You make me this way?" Can the clay say to the potter, "Why did you make me this way?" (see Romans 9:20).

> "What sorrow awaits those who argue with their Creator. Does a clay pot argue with its maker? Does the clay dispute with the one who shapes it, saying, 'Stop, you're doing it wrong!' Does the pot exclaim, 'How clumsy can you be?'" (Isaiah 45:9 NLT).

When we surrender to the lordship of Jesus Christ, through the power of the Holy Spirit we move beyond just functioning in society and arguing with our creator to thriving as we are transformed and our minds renewed and restored to wholeness.

The Holy Spirit walked me through step by step of breaking free from debilitating behaviors by letting go of the hurt, trauma, and my own sinful past, covered by the blood of Jesus and the washing of His Word through sanctification. He led me to a place of knowing God's love was sufficient for everything I ever needed or faced. He taught me how to embrace His love, how to love myself and others above the pain and hurt in my heart. My desire for belonging was complete when I came into the family of God. "For you have been born again. Your new life did not come from your earthly parents because the life they gave you will end in death. But this new life will last forever because it comes from the eternal, living word of God" (1 Peter 1:23 NLT).

> "His unchanging plan has always been to adopt us into his own family by bringing us to himself through Jesus Christ. And this gave him great pleasure" (Ephesians 1:5 NLT).

When we belong to God's family, He changes us from the inside out to bring us to wholeness and the purpose for which He designed us to carry out.

The Lord put on my heart to write a Bible Study Book that walks you through this journey of self-discovery and Spiritual Growth. Discovering Your Spiritual DNA is available on Amazon and my website www.narrowgatenow.com.

RESTORED TO PURPOSE:

"For we are His workmanship created in Christ Jesus for good works, which God prepared beforehand that we should walk in them" (Ephesians 2:10 NKJV).

We're restored to our true selves, our life's calling, forever free from the false personas we created for ourselves by trying to please others to cope with living in a corrupt, fallen, and sinful world. This is what God has been waiting to reveal to us from the beginning.

"If anyone is in Christ, he is a new creature; the old has gone and the new has come!" (2 Corinthians 5:17 NIV).

The change that happens in you after surrendering your life to Christ is undeniable.

If no one else can perceive it, God does, and He is well pleased. You will have confirmation of the change in you as healing and restoration take form. Circumstances that once had control over your thought process revealed through your behavior and anxious reactions no longer have the same effect on you. When things aren't going the way you thought they should, you're no longer responding by throwing childish tantrums because you now have a way of expressing your anger and emotions from a biblical lens through the power of the Holy Spirit living in you. You're holding your tongue, rather than letting it burn fires. You're maturing in Christ! You're guarding your heart.

"Above all else, guard your heart, for everything you do flows from it" (Proverbs 4:23 NIV). "The fruit of the Spirit is now permeating your being, and you can't even believe it yourself. But the fruit of the Spirit is love, joy, peace, longsuffering, kindness, goodness, faithfulness, gentleness, self-control. Against such there is no law" (Galatians 5:22-23 NKJV). This is an ongoing process as you move forward in your surrendered life from glory to glory. We are healed and restored to go out and share the Good News about how you can have a new life in Christ!

Here are some questions to ponder on your personal journey of healing and restoration.

- Interruptions: When they come unexpectedly, do you still have Peace?
- Delays: When you can't control it, do you still have Patience?
- Insults: When you've done nothing to deserve it, do you still have Joy?
- Offenses: When they're not doing what they said they would, are you still Loving?
- How are you exhibiting and sharing the fruits of the Spirit in your life?
- Are you loving God, yourself, and others?

"Love suffers long and is kind; love does not envy; love does not parade itself, is not puffed up; does not behave rudely, does not seek its own, is not provoked, thinks no evil; does not rejoice in iniquity, but rejoices in the truth; bears all things, believes all things, hopes all things, endures all things. Love never fails" (1 Corinthians 13:4-8a NKJV).

CHAPTER TEN
MOVING FORWARD SURRENDERED

STAY SURRENDERED TO live the life God designed for you to live! In the book of John, Jesus says, "Apart from me you can do nothing. I am the vine; you are the branches. He who abides in Me, and I in Him, bears much fruit; for without Me you can do nothing" (John 15:5 NKJV).

We need to remember this because apart from Jesus we can do nothing.

Keep moving, seeking, reaching, growing, finding, loving, and embracing the things of God, and take it into the world (your job, grocery store, neighborhood, school, etc.) where the Lord has placed you as Christ's ambassador.

"For God was in Christ, reconciling the world to himself, no longer counting people's sins against them. This is the wonderful message he has given us to tell others. We are Christ's ambassadors" (2 Corinthians 5:19-20a NLT).

In Chapter 2, I mentioned a Christian owned business who gave me 10k to sell their services, to which I defaulted. In September of 2020, I met with the owner and his colleagues, repented and returned the money with interest. There was no legal contract for me to do so, it was the Holy Spirit and a testimony of my surrendered life.

> "If anyone would come after me, he must deny himself and take up his cross and follow me. For whoever wants to save his life will lose it, but whoever loses his life for me will find it" (Matthew 16:24-25 NIV).

It's no longer I who live but Christ in me. As Paul writes, "I have been crucified with Christ; it is no longer I who live, but Christ lives in me and the life which I now live in the flesh I live by faith in the Son of God, who loved me and gave Himself for me" (Galatians 2:20 NKJV).

This is not just for Paul, apostles, prophets, evangelists, pastors, and teachers; this is for all of us who have the Spirit of the Lord living in them or who desire to have the Spirit of the Lord living in them.

When I awake in the morning, the first thing I usually say is, "Thank you, Lord, for another day to grow in faith." As I shared, in a previous chapter, early on in my walk, the Lord spoke to me and said, "Plan as if you are going to live 100 years, but live each day as if it were your last." From that day on, I began living my daily life with this in mind. The Bible is clear that we have today; tomorrow is promised to no one. So, what are you going to do with today? Ask the Lord and receive your answer! Stay connected through prayer, the Holy Spirit, God's Word, and God's people, trusting the Lord to move you forward from glory to glory.

Stay connected...

THROUGH PRAYER:

Have you heard it said, "Well, I have done all I could do, the only thing I have left to do is pray"? That is good, but I would suggest praying first, then doing what you can do and praying again! Start with prayer for everything you need, every issue you face, and thankfulness for all God has done for you! Prayer is our connection to the heavenly realm. It is Heaven's phone number.

You may think to yourself, "Sometimes I don't even know what to pray." God has you covered. When we do not know what to pray, the Word tells us that the Holy Spirit prays on our behalf.

THE HOLY SPIRIT:

"The Holy Spirit helps us in our weakness. For example, we don't know what God wants us to pray for. But the Holy Spirit prays for us with groanings that cannot be expressed in words. And the Father who knows all hearts knows what the Spirit is saying, for the Spirit pleads for us believers in harmony with God's own will" (Romans 8:26-27 NLT). All the more reason to stay connected to the Holy Spirit. Go where the Holy Spirit leads, even if it does not make sense to you. Go!

Jesus promised the Holy Spirit would be sent to us to lead us into all truth. This is not only the truth of the Gospel, but the truth of who we were created to be. The Holy Spirit will lead us there. He will lead you to where you need to read in the Word, the people you need to be connected to, and the next step you need to take.

"However, when He, the Spirit of truth has come, He will guide you into all truth; for He will not speak on His own authority, but whatever He hears He will speak; and He will tell you things to come" (John 16:13 NKJV).

The Holy Spirit will lead you down the path the Lord designed uniquely for you. Our job is to stay connected and obedient to the Holy Spirit's leading and receive by faith what the Father has prepared for us before the foundations of the world through Jesus Christ. We have to submit to the sanctification process by the Holy Spirit to be separated from the sin in our being if we desire to live the life that Jesus died for us to have. The sanctification process may vary, but the outcome is the same. Separation from sin unto holiness! The more of the Word you get in you, the easier it will be.

GOD'S WORD:

"Sanctify them by Your truth. Your Word is truth. As You sent Me into the world, I also have sent them into the world. And for their sakes I sanctify Myself, that they also may be sanctified by the truth" (John 17:17-19 NKJV).

"I do not pray for these alone, but also for those who will believe in Me through their word" (John 17:20 NKJV).

Wow, Jesus was praying not only for His disciples then, but for us now, today! The Word of God is alive and is the power source to transform our lives and keep us transformed. Our flesh has the inclination to slip back into our old ways. Our subconscious mind wants to keep us in our established comfort zones, but God wants more for our lives, and it can only be accomplished as we continue feeding our souls and spirit with His Word!

I heard a preacher early on say, "This book (the Bible) will keep you from sin, or sin will keep you from this book." You will have to discipline yourself to get into the Word every day! If you're not inclined to get in the Word daily, pray about it, and ask other believers to pray with you for a breakthrough.

GOD'S PEOPLE

One time when Jesus was teaching, He was told that His mother and brothers were outside looking to speak with Him. But He replied, "'Who is My mother and who are My brothers?' And He stretched out His hand toward His disciples and said, 'Here are My mother and My brothers! For whoever does the will of My Father in heaven is My brother and sister and mother'" (Matthew 12:48-50 NKJV).

You need to know who you are surrounding yourself with, including your immediate family, a potential mate or spouse, and the church you are attending. From the pastor on down, you need to know not only what they profess to believe but what they practice. Find out what is in their heart by asking God.

Only God knows the true heart of a man! Let the Holy Spirit lead you to the church you should attend, the friendships you should embrace, and the relationships in which you should engage. I often tell my daughters that whenever you come to a place where you think you're ready to start a relationship toward marriage, you need to pray and ask the Lord, "Is this the man that you have for me?" It does not matter how good-looking a person is or how nice they appear, even if the person is in the church or pulpit. We all have issues to work through, and you need to know if this is the person that the Lord has graced you to walk alongside in sickness and in health, for richer or poorer, and in good times and in bad. The Bible clearly says bad company corrupts good character.

"Don't be fooled by those who say such things, for 'bad company corrupts good character'" (1 Corinthians 15:33 NLT).

The Bible says you will know them by their fruit, and this takes time. You really do not know someone until you are in a close relationship with them. The closest being a spouse, but also a co-worker, friend, and confidant, when their true behavior and motives are evident through day-to-day interactions. The true measure of the heart of a man is how he responds when he is not getting his way.

When I met my husband after going through a previous divorce, I was extremely cautious. The Holy Spirit walked me through step by step. I remember one day when he came in to visit from Nashville. I prayed and asked the Lord, "What does he want from me?" The Holy Spirit spoke in my spirit and said, "He just wants to be with you!" He had no ulterior motives. This was music to my ears and a joy to my heart! I remember after he left when the weekend was over, I prayed and said, "Lord, I will walk through whatever it is that you would have me to walk through with him." I was committed on that day!

A few months later when I got enough courage to travel to Nashville to his home I learned more about him. I witnessed his response to unjust behavior and was overjoyed with the heart of this man. He never withdrew from his responsibilities, as countless others may have. I told him, I am sorry these things happened in your life, but I am glad to see the man you are by how you have handled it through your continued dedication and support of your family. So, likewise, without hesitation, he stepped up into the role of husband and stepfather to provide and protect where it was needed for my three daughters and myself. We have had challenges to endure, but when Christ is in the center of your life and your house is built on the Rock, it will still be standing when everything is being shaken. Christ the solid rock on which we stand!

You should also surround yourself with accountability partners, your spouse, and/or other trusted believers from a Bible study or small group with whom you can walk closely. Someone you can mutually rely upon to point out your areas of difficulty or blindness, and who can offer constructive criticism where it is needed, support during difficult times, and acceptance of who you are and where you are in your spiritual journey.

Keep in mind, a person can appear as if they have surrendered their life to the lordship of Jesus Christ. But the truth is found in the motives of the person's heart. Going to church, praying, operating in your spiritual gifting, giving to the poor, tithing, and other similar activities may be good, but they are not the key factors on whether a person is truly surrendered. Consider this scripture: "Not all people who sound religious are really godly. They may refer to me as 'Lord,' but they still won't enter the Kingdom of Heaven. The decisive issue is whether they obey my Father in heaven. On judgment day many will tell me, 'Lord, Lord we prophesied in your name and cast out demons in your name and performed many miracles in your name.' But I will reply, 'I never knew you. Go away, the things you did were unauthorized'" (Matthew 7:21-23 NLT).

How will you know the truth? "Jesus said to the people who believed in him, 'You are truly my disciples if you keep obeying my teachings. And you will know the truth and the truth will set you free'" (John 8:31-32 NLT). These are good scriptures to examine your heart about whether or not you are truly surrendered. If you have any doubts, repent, and ask the Holy Spirit to reveal areas in your life where you need to repent and surrender.

Trust in the Lord to move you forward from glory to glory.

We have a role to play and that's moving forward where the Lord is leading.

If you have not already received the baptism of the Holy Spirit with evidence of speaking in tongues, then pray for it. Go to a believer who has it, and ask them to pray over you and lay hands on you to receive your spiritual language. Follow their lead as they pray in tongues, and let the Holy Spirit give you your prayer language. Praying for the baptism in the Holy Spirit empowers you to walk out your calling with divine power from above, no matter where you are on the job, in church, school, or on the road. Pray and receive it!

Q: What is God's will for your life?

A: That you surrender your life completely to Him.

Surrender now! It is available for you! Start today to enjoy your new adventure of living completely for Christ! My prayer for you and all the people you will touch is that you will choose to completely surrender!

Pray this prayer of surrender or something similar:

> Heavenly Father, I surrender now to the lordship of Jesus Christ in every area of my life. I will submit to following the Holy Spirit. Help me, Lord, to honor You in everything I do and go through, knowing You have the best plan for my life here on earth and into eternity. I pray for strength, courage, and perseverance to walk where You would have me to walk, to say what You would have me say, and to do what You would have me to do in my personal life, work life, church life, and every area of my life. I ask this in Jesus' name, Amen!

ACKNOWLEDGMENTS

To God, who gave His Word, and Jesus who went to the cross and prepared a pathway for me to come to full surrender through the power of the Holy Spirit!

To my husband, I love you deeply! Thank you for believing and validating the gifts the Lord has put in me, and for supporting and encouraging me to flourish in what the Lord has called me to do. To my daughters, I love all three of you beyond measure! Thank you for loving me in the good and difficult times! For inspiring me without knowing to surrender, stand for truth, and leave a spiritual legacy for you and your children's children.

To my family, friends and spiritual mentors, thank you for your encouragement and for coming alongside me through this journey. I'm forever grateful! A special thanks to James Goll and his team for writing, How to Write Book, a prophetic online book writing class, which gave me the tools needed to complete Surrendered. To Tall Pine Books for their exemplary publishing work and spiritual insight for the advancement of Kingdom purposes.

To the Christian women of AWSA (Advanced Writers and Speakers Association) who provided priceless wisdom and knowledge in completing my final edits of Surrendered.

To the deliverance ministers, especially Pastor Greg Locke, who exposed the infiltration of the demonic realm within the church, and to the Prophets who prophetically spoke of the remnant being raised up for such a time as this, on Christian Television, radio, and social media. Especially, The Voice of the Prophets, on the PTL network, The Jim Bakker Show. I'm thankful to all of them, as it has empowered me to be fearless in what the Lord called me to do and get this book to market!

Thank you for purchasing my book, as a special offer when you become a subscriber you will receive our newsletter and other discounts.

To become a subscriber, go to www.narrowgatenow.com, on the home page.

God bless you,

Debra Elrod

REFERENCES

- The Word of God – Jesus Christ
- My personal testimony - (Rev. 12:11 NKJV)
- Holy Spirit Revelation – (1 John 2:27 NLT)
- Scripture, Bible Verses derived from:
  New Living Translation, Tyndale Publishing 1996.
  New International Version, Zondervan Publishing 2001
  New King James Version, Holman Publishers, 2013
  King James Version, Hendrickson Publishers, 2009
  Amplified Bible, The Bible App.
- Discovering Your Spiritual DNA, A complete guide to changing your thinking and transforming your life. A comprehensive Bible Study, Debra A. Elrod, Tall Pine Books publications (2023)

ABOUT THE AUTHOR

DEBRA ELROD is a Surrendered Believer, Bible teacher, leader, Founder and Executive Director of Narrow Gate Now Ministries, Inc. www.narrowgatenow.com; teaching Biblical Business Principals in the marketplace. She is President of Propel Industries, Inc. a business development firm. She obtained a Bachelor of Science degree in Business, specializing in Marketing/Advertising and Public Relations in 1993 and is a Veteran of the U.S. Army, Honorably Discharged in 1992. On December 7, 2005, she had a radical encounter with the God of the universe that transformed her life forever. She went from religious darkness to the Kingdom of light, led by the Holy Spirit. She has since dedicated her life to speaking the Truth and sharing the Truth of the Word, wherever the Holy Spirit leads as a follower of Jesus Christ.

STUDY QUESTIONS

CHAPTER ONE

- What role does seeking God with all your heart play in discovering God's will for your life, as mentioned in Jeremiah 29:13 and Matthew 7:7-8? How does this relate to surrender?
- What are some noticeable changes in a person's life that can occur once they have surrendered to God? How does the Holy Spirit influence these changes?

CHAPTER TWO

- What role does the Holy Spirit play in guiding and directing a person's life? How is this guidance in line with the Word of God?
- Chapter Two discusses the idea of allowing the Holy Spirit to expose hidden wounds and lies in one's soul. Why is this important, and how can one go about allowing the Holy Spirit to work in this way?

CHAPTER THREE

- Why is obedience considered a critical component in one's spiritual journey? How does obedience relate to receiving what God has prepared for us?
- Chapter Three emphasizes the importance of transformation in one's mind through obedience to God's Word. Can you share a personal experience where obedience to God's Word led to a transformation in your thinking or behavior?

CHAPTER FOUR

- What are "quiet times" in the context of chapter four, and why are they important for a Christian's spiritual growth?
- In what ways can quiet times be a period of renewal and refreshing for a believer? How does the Holy Spirit play a role in this renewal process?

CHAPTER FIVE

- Why is faith considered essential for pleasing God, and how does faith connect us to God's rewards, according to Hebrews 11:6?

- The chapter mentions four types of faith tests: belief tests, waiting tests, trust tests, and love tests. Explain each type and provide examples of how these tests can manifest in our lives.

CHAPTER SIX

- What role does the Holy Spirit play in helping individuals find freedom from mental and spiritual strongholds?
- What is the author's definition of "true freedom" as described in the chapter, and how does it differ from conventional notions of freedom?

CHAPTER SEVEN

- How does knowing your identity in Christ influence your behavior and relationships, especially when it comes to apologizing for wrongdoing and setting healthy boundaries?
- The chapter emphasizes the concept of righteousness through faith in Christ's sacrifice. How does this concept differ from relying on one's own actions to attain righteousness before God?

CHAPTER EIGHT

- What is the significance of going through "tribulation valley" when surrendering and walking with Jesus? How does it differ for each person?
- When we surrender to Jesus, the enemy may wage attacks against us. How can believers prepare themselves to face these attacks, and what role does faith play in overcoming them?

CHAPTER NINE

- What are the key components of healing, deliverance, and restoration in the Christian journey?
- What role do repentance and love play as anchors for one's spiritual journey?

CHAPTER TEN

- What does Jesus' statement in John 15:5 ("Apart from me you can do nothing") mean in the context of surrendering to God's plan for your life, and how does it relate to staying connected to Him?
- In Matthew 16:24-25, Jesus talks about denying oneself and taking up one's cross to follow Him. How does this teaching align with the idea of surrendering to God's will, and what does it mean for us today?

Index